Chiel o' the

C000116664

An Aberlady Boyhood
1862 - 1877

by

John Pringle Reid

Chiel o' the Clachan

An Aberlady Boyhood
1862 – 1877

by

John Pringle Reid

Transcribed and Edited by
Ian Malcolm

Illustrated by Sally J Collins

Chapter I

I am now in my eighteenth year, and, though I haven't seen or come through any more, very likely not so much, as the generality of laddies of my age, still, I've made up my mind to write a bit history of my own life such as it is. For all the millions of folk who inhabit this globe, though every one were to write their own life, it would be found that there were not two alike; so mine, though there is nothing very interesting or wonderful about it, will, in some way or other differ, from other folk's. But if every one who had as little to write about as I, were to do it, there would be an immense number of autobiographies not worth the reading. Therefore, it is not because I think my life is more worth writing about, or that I have more ability to write it than my neighbours, but simply for the following reasons. First, now that the long nights of winter are fast approaching, and having the remainder of the night after five o'clock to myself, it will keep me from wearying; and at the same time keep me from doing worse. Second, it may help to improve my handwriting, which is anything but what I would like it to be. And third, it will bring back to mind the happy days of auld lang syne; not that I can say I am anything else but happy now-a-days; but still, they are not the days o' auld lang syne -

"Aft, aft have I ponder'd on scenes o' my
  childhood,
Thae days ance sae happy, Oh
  come back again!
When I pu'd the wild daisies that
  spangled the greenwood,
And gied them awa' tae my wee
  lovers then,
Oh, memories dear!"

It will be observed that I am using our own national dialect; but I fear I am not master enough of it to do it justice, as us Scottish youths now-a-days have little chance to be thoroughly acquainted with the language of our forebears. I am sad, sad to see how rapidly the English language is supplanting the good 'braid auld Scottish tongue', and that our countrymen have so far forgot themselves as to encourage it! If fortune or pleasure should induce any of our Scotch folk to make a tour into the Southern country, and it be their lot to stay there a while; when again they return to their native land, it is nine chances to one they'll have banished their own Doric dialect, and be speaking that High English, Queen's English, or whatever they like to call it. And not content with that, but they will ridicule, or try to do it rather, the good, simple, and expressive language of their ancestors as a "coarse, vulgar and unintelligible tongue altogether." Others again, themselves above the commonality, or are getting up in the world, as far as wealth and pride

1

are concerned, forsake their mother tongue, and such as it is 'not for any polished society or any well-bred person whomsoever'. What base, absurd ideas! Fit only for the contempt of every genuine Scotsman. Nevertheless, it seems inevitable, that in two or three centuries after this, if the world should hold out that time, the Scottish language will cease to be spoken, or even understood; when the majority of the works of Burns and other great and noble Scotsmen will be given to antiquarians as samples of a language once spoken by the people in the Lowlands of Scotland.

Chapter II

Before I begin to relate the bits of incidents of my youthful life, it beholds me to describe, to the best of my small ability, the place where I was born and brought up.

Aberlady is a parish on the north-west coast of the county of Haddington, and contains a post-office village of the same name. Its greatest dimension is about four miles in a line running from north-east to south-west, and is nearly three miles in a line running north and south. It is in general very level, and, I may safely say, one of the most fertile parishes in Scotland. The population is a little above 1,000, of which number the village can claim about 480.

The Peffer Burn, which was once called the Ledie (whence the name of the place), and is the north-east boundary of the parish, rising in the parish of Athelstaneford and after a winding course of seven miles empties its waters (which are but small) into the Firth of Forth near the village of Aberlady. The village lies on the Firth which here forms Aberlady Bay, and is five miles north-west of Haddington, and fifteen to the east of Edinburgh on the road to North Berwick. It doesn't belong to the kind of Scottish villages as described in Mrs Hamilton's *"Cottagers of Glenburnie"* and in other books, as consisting of a row of low, dirty hovels, each one having a broken cart at the side of the door, a dung-hill at the other, and a washing basket in front, with, the broken panes of the windows stuffed with straw, etc.; but is, as the most of the villages hereabouts are, a bonnie, clean-looking place. It consists of one pretty long street, and a lane or by-street running down to the sea-side called 'the Wynd', the latter being perhaps an exception to the general cleanliness. The former, however, is a wide, open street, of a rather picturesque appearance, the most of the houses having a piece of ground before their doors filled according to the taste of their inhabitants; some with turf and trees or shrubs, others with flowers of many varieties, and in the whole being enclosed within a small dyke and railing. At the back of each house, again, is generally a good big garden containing fruit trees, vegetables, and flowers. There are two Kirks, an Established at the west end, and a U.P. in the Wynd; there is also a school, with a good attendance, in the middle of the village. Along by the sea-side is a track of fine, short grass, varying from about fifty to one hundred yards in breadth, which affords a splendid recreation ground for the youngsters of the village; and I think I need not hesitate in saying that there I've spent the happiest days of my life. To the north-west of the village into some small banks and braes which in the summer months are covered with daisies, buttercups, craw-toes, etc., aft have I

> "ran aboot the braes,
> And pu'd the gowans fine;
> But mony a weary fit I've trod
> Sin' the days o' auld langsyne."

I only need to look to the Peffer Burn and add that I

> "hae paddled in yon burn
> Frae mornin' sun till dine.
> Ah, yes! but these are departed joys,
> Departed ne'er to return."

Aberlady bay is left dry (save the Peffer Burn which runs through it) when the tide is out, and is then a wide expanse of sands abounding in cockles, spouts, spout-mothers and other shell-fish. The rocks that are covered when the sea is in, afford a habitation for mussels, wilks, limpets, and what not.

About a mile and a half west of the village is Gosford House, the seat of the Earl of Wemyss and March. The late Earl built a splendid mansion here, but as the stones were of a damp nature, it has never been inhabited. The grounds round about it are very bonnie - well I'll not spoil them trying to describe them; but I am sorry to say the public are now entirely excluded from getting a sight of them.

At a shorter distance to the east of the village is Luffness House, a fine old mansion, belonging to W.H. Hope Esquire. Near it are the remains of a Bickerton in a conventual building that belonged to the Carmelites.

In the field behind the Established Kirk and manse may be seen all that is left of Kilspindie, where at a very early date the Culdees had a seat. About the end of the fifteenth century Kilspindie was the abode of a favourite courtier of James IV, called Spens, who was renowned for his chivalry and had defied the haughty Earl of Angus, head of the Douglases, while at court. A short time after Angus met Spens near Borthwick in the county of Edinburgh, he slew him after a fierce encounter, then fled to his castle of Hermitage in Liddesdale, where he remained till the anger of the king was abated. During the minority of James V, the Earl of Angus, grandson and a successor to him who killed Spens, was regent, and his uncle Sir Archibald Douglas, the high-treasurer was in possession of Kilspindie, though 'hoo it cam' I ne'er kent yet'. However, when the King got the government into his own hands, the Douglases were banished from the country for their treasonable actions; Angus and his brother Sir George Douglas fled into England, and Sir Archibald Douglas of Kilspindie to France. Although the latter had taken no forward part in the aggrandising and treasonable plans of his nephews during the minority of the King, still he was a Douglas, and was banished along with them who deserved it. Getting tired of his exile in France, and seized with a strong longing for home, Sir Archibald, who was now an old man, minding the King's personal attachment to him, resolved to return to Scotland and seek royal forgiveness. As the King was returning from Stirling after a hunting expedition, the banished earl threw himself in his way, but James, mindful of his oath that he would never let a Douglas find refuge in Scotland, passed on without taking notice of him; and though Douglas, in spite of the heavy armour that he wore, ran by the side of the King's horse to the palace gates he failed to get a word from his implacable master. He sat down at the gate weary and exhausted, and when he asked for a drink of water even this was refused by the royal attendants; and he was compelled to return to France, where, in a short time, he died of a broken heart. Although I am almost sure this is the Kilspindie, yet it might be that in Perthshire which belonged to the Douglases.

At one time smuggling had been pretty freely carried on hereabouts; there are two caves within a short distance of the village, and there is an old house at the foot of the Wynd in which there is a concealed press and other things that would mostly prove that at one time its inhabitants were dealers in contraband goods.

But, that is Aberlady in the past; it is now a very quiet place, and turning a very fashionable resort for sea-bathers in the summer months.

Chapter III

Almost opposite the head of the Wynd is a shop occupied by the proprietor Mr Hunter, who carries on the business of a baker, there having been a bakehouse lately built on the premises. However, in the year 1861 James Reid, photographer, who also carried on the grocery trade, tenanted this shop. He was at this time a widower left with three daughters, the youngest of them about nine years old. His father also lived in Aberlady and faithfully discharged his duty as doctor to the village and surrounding district.

A rumour was abroad that James Reid was, in a short time, to be married to Mary Pringle, a milliner and dressmaker in the village, and whose father was, or had been, a farmer at Ballencrieff Mains, a farm about a mile and a quarter out of the village. But, in country places rumours like that, very often little truth in them,

4

being almost made up by each person adding a wee bit of their own fancy to anything they hear. For instance: a young couple taking a walk together may be seen by a laddie, who'll go and tell the first old wife he meets, that he saw Mr Such-a-body walking with Miss Such-another-body and that they looked very friendly like. This old wife most likely would tell some other one that she heard M^r S- was going with Miss S- and that it looked like they were engaged. This one in her turn would tell, perhaps a young wife this time that M^r S- and Miss S- were engaged and they would likely be married soon. And lastly, when this young wife's man comes home from his work at night she will ask, "Did you hear Mr Such-a-body was tae be married tae Miss Such-anither-body?"

"No!"

"I believe it's quite true though."

So there it is spouted over all the countryside that that couple are to be married, although they would perhaps never think of meeting again. Nevertheless, though rumours in many cases may be false, in this one it was true enough as James Reid and Mary Pringle were married in the autumn of that year. And now, with the aid of his wife, James Pringle added to his business that of a draper.

'Twas on the longest day (21st June) of the year 1862, it happened to be a Saturday, that Dr Reid, when coming out his son's house, met a woman whom he told he had that day got a grandson. "Oh, ho!" she exclaimed, "that'll be twa births in Aberlady the-day. Nae aften that happens, an' baith laddies tae."

"Aye", replied the doctor, "an' baith daein' weel."

The other woman who had got a son that day was Mrs Bathgate, a forester's wife, living at the east end of the village. The former laddie was myself, James Reid, my father, and Dr Reid, my grandfather. No doubt, I would get my hugging and 'hushie-ba' from a wider circle of females than that of our own family; and each one would be saying I was like some friend or other, or find something wonderful about me. Then they would foretell what I was to be - a photographer, like my father, a doctor, like my grandfather, or some of them would perhaps go the length of saying, "He'll wag his heid in a poopit yet." But, among all their prophesying, I'll warrant there was no-one who guessed what I am, at this day at any rate. I lived and thrived and grew a sturdy fellow, of which both father and mother would doubtless be very proud and, when I was old enough to be taken to the Kirk, I was christened John Pringle. However, a change very soon came over the scene. Long before I discovered which end of me was upmost, or had got a glimpse of the imperfectabilities of my sinful nature, I had the great misfortune to lose my mother. Many a one mourned her untimely death, for, as I have often been told,

5

she was an amiable, devout woman. My father was again a widower, and again his joy turned into mourning. But still I lived and thrived, chiefly owing to the good nursing and good sweet milk, both of which I would get plenty of; the latter was obtained from Luffness Mains, a farm fully a mile from the village.

Time rolled on, and in two years my father was again married. His bride this time was Margaret Brown from the village of Slateford, near Edinburgh. For this step I have much reason to be very thankful. My step-mother's mother and niece came shortly after this, so that at the time our household were, my father and mother, my eldest sister Chrisie, my second, Mary, my youngest, Maggie, Mrs Brown, my grandmother, and Maggie Horsburgh, my cousin, and myself - who I was very near forgetting - not often that's the case you'll be thinking.

Chapter IV

I now begin to relate those incidents that have a place in my memory. When my present mother came I was a wee above two years old, and not long after that I achieved the first great exploit that I mind of, which was to set the chimney on fire.

This chimney, which was the backshop one, had a big bend in it, and each time it was sooted, the soot, instead of coming right down, had accumulated in the bend, till it amounted to perhaps two or three barrowful. It happened one day when my mother was cooking some fat, savoury meat, that I, either drawn by the good smell or some other temptation got to the fireside also; and while there somebody came into the shop whom my mother had to attend, thus leaving me alone by the fire-side. My very first thought was to see what was getting ready for dinner and, while trying to satisfy my inquisitiveness, I knocked over the pot or pan, whatever it was, and help! It went up in a blaze such as I had never seen before or have ever seen yet inside a house; the soot took hold, and the chimney was soon roaring like a tremendous tempest through a huge forest. First came my mother who turned as white as a cloth when she saw what was what, and could do neither one thing nor another. Then came the rest of the family, but they just stood in one another's way. Some, however, began to bring the water and pour it in the fire; others went to alarm the neighbours; and the house was, in a short time, a scene of the upmost confusion and alarm. "What's tae be done?" was the general cry "that bend i' the lum has taen haud, an' the hoose'll aiblins be burnt tae the grund afore a's done." Ay! 'What was to be done' was a question, which no one there could answer, except only with no effect. By this time the chimney looked like it would fall in; and shortly the flames broke through and burnt some things. But, this was its worst, and it gradually became less, though it wasn't right out twenty-four hours after the beginning of it. A good deal less damage was done than expected; although there was quite enough for all that and there will be a good many folk in

Aberlady who'll mind about it as a narrow escape of the house being burnt. Now that the fire was over, my father had plenty of time to give me due admonition for my mischief, while my mother and the rest of the household were very glad it was all by, and that it had been no worse.

Since ever I could toddle about outside the doors, and observe the objects that were to be seen there, the ponies, horses, and other quadrupeds took up a good deal of my attention; and I became very desirous to get a pony of my own. The ways in which I tried to get one always make me laugh when I think of them. In addition to what I have already related about my father, he was an artist; he was a joiner to trade, keeping his hand in by making odds and ends for the house and shop, when he would very often have me as an interested spectator; he also did a bit at the gardening as most men in villages like Aberlady do, keeping their own gardens in order; many other things he did that are needless to mention. I begged daily at him to make me a pony, which he in time did; it was a wooden one with a little hair nailed on for a tail, bits of leather for ears, and buttons stuck into its face for eyes. This diverted me for a wee while, but it was a living one I wanted.

In those days, when it was time for me go to my bed, my mother used to say as a bit of encouragement, "Noo, Johnnie ye'll gang awa' tae yer bed, an' sleep for siller to buy a coo." That was well enough, but if she had said "siller to buy a pownie", she might have got me to sleep long enough. My wooden pony I soon got tired of: I would take it to a place where there was plenty of good grass and would pull some and push it into its mouth, but it wouldn't eat at all: I gave it a tinful of fine clear water but it wouldn't drink either; so I thought I must get one that can eat and drink and give me a ride when I wanted it. An idea struck me how I could get it. I pulled the tail off my wooden pony, and planted it in the garden, as I had seen my father do the potatoes, thinking it would grow into a living one; but each time I would look to see it coming up, nothing was to be seen, and I dug where I had planted and there was the hair as I had put it in. My grievances I made known to some of the younger members of the family, who told me that if I got some hair off a living pony and planted it, it would grow the same as the one I had got it off. On the sea-side green there grazed an old Shetland beastie called Donald that was very cannie, and would let the laddies do mostly anything to it; so there I ran and got a big handful of Donald's hair (there being always plenty hanging loose about him) and went straight to the garden where I planted it, leaving a wee bit sticking up as I had been told to do. Every morning when I went to see it, to my great satisfaction and joy, it had grown up about an inch further than the preceding morning (somebody had got there before me and pulled it up a wee bit). One morning, however, it was up altogether and blown very near to the other end of the garden, it being very windy that day, just at a time when I was expecting to see the back legs coming up, as I thought it would grow tail foremost. This was a sore stroke to me, and put an end to my endeavours at growing ponies, and to my

7

notion of them altogether, I think, for after that there was never a whisper about one again.

Chapter V

My bad memory forces me to skip over the next two years of my life without saying anything about them, as I mind of nothing exceptional happening then. But, I must say that during that time I grew very fast and thoroughly enjoyed my life's early morn.

I was now about five years old, and sometimes overheard the very unwelcome news that "Johnnie will sune need tae gang tae the schule noo". Yes, far over soon that day came, when I was taken from my sweet sunny rambles by the sea-side, and sent off to the school with a slate by my side, and an "A.B.C." in my hand. Och on! I never liked the school at all; as I daresay my grammar and composition will be quite sufficient proof. At first, I was mostly under the tuition of an Aunt, the female and only assistant in the Aberlady school, who faithfully discharges that duty until this day; and though not favoured any more than my mates, it sort of helped to make me reconciled to my lot. I don't rightly mind whether I got on well with my lessons or not, but I know very well that I soon came to learn what the belt was; for, as I was very inattentive, I got my share of what was going. One day, however, at dinner-time, I took it into my head not to return to the school that day, so I found out a hidie-hole where I comfortably took up my abode for the time being. Shortly, I heard one of my schoolmates in the house speaking with my mother; he had been sent by the master to see what had kept me from the school, but as they couldn't find me anywhere he had to go back as wise as he came. Whenever his back was turned, and all things seemed quiet, I tripped out and enjoyed myself the rest of the day. At night, when I went home, neither my father nor mother said much about it; but my faith not so the master when I reappeared next day! That was the first time, but not the last, I played the truant from the school.

In the year 1868, and on the May term of that year, we flitted from the house opposite the head of the Wynd to the one now occupied by Mrs Welsh, near the middle of the village, and right opposite the school. Although I would, no doubt, be very vexed to leave the house in which I had been born, and had spent so many happy days, and also our honest and kind neighbours - M^r and Mrs Adam - yet I'm very sure I did rejoice in the fact that I didn't need to go to the school, that day at any rate. Early in the morning, hearing all the din and hullo-bulloo in the house, I got up out of my bed and down the stair, where I beheld more confusion and turmoil than I've ever seen, that day I set the chimney on fire not excepted. There was a hurrying within the house, and a running up the stair, and a running down the stair; a packing up, and a carrying out; while every now and then would be heard a dunt, as some larger piece of furniture would come in contact with the wall, or as the bearers thereof would lay it down to rest their well-tried muscles; and numerous other well-known attendants on flittings. Then, the cart packed, the men would follow it up to our future dwelling where the things were unpacked, and put in the most convenient places, etc., etc.

During all this hurry-burry it is not to be expected that I would get leave, or yet seek leave, to remain "a calm spectator merely", no, no! You may be sure I was very busy, in my way, carrying some of the smaller articles to our new house, and rejoicing all the time at the happy contrast between that job and my school lessons. More than that, I flatter myself I had not the heaviest or yet the most awkward piece of furniture, but yet what I consider would be the most difficult to flit of all - namely, the cat. Long had I to watch for the opportunity of getting pussie shut into a room, when a basket had to be procured, into which I had no small difficulty in getting her, not before she had gave some fierce yowls and a few scratches too; then when I thought her all safe and before I could get the lid fastened she forced her way out, and was again running round the room, this making her all the more difficult to secure the second time. At last, however, I got puss all right into the basket, thence I proceeded up the village (the yowls attracting a number of bairns to my side, who enjoyed a good deal of fun at my expense), and put the astonished cat into the kitchen of the new house, where she got some tasty bit of meat in order to make her a wee bit more satisfied with her lot. But, the first opportunity the cat could get she didn't hesitate in returning to her old abode, where I followed and had again to go through the performance of catching and bringing home that useful animal. Yet that wasn't all, for puss was as determined to stay in her former home as we were that she should stay in her new one; so it wasn't before she had been three or four times flitted that she became reconciled to her fate, and made a permanent stop in our new residence.

In a wonderful short time all things were put to right; and I, at least, soon forgot that I hadn't lived there all my days.

Chapter VI

Now almost twelve months have flown away to 'the tomb o' the unburied past' since I wrote the preceding chapters, and I fear, I have lost the thread of my story altogether; in fact, I don't mind what I was going to say at all. Nevertheless, as I like not to begin a thing and not finish it, I will try and carry on my autobiography to the best of my limited ability.

Our new house and shop was the property of a Mr Simpson who lived in the next house to the west of ours - I say was the property as it has just been sold to the Earl of Wemyss, the former proprietor being now deceased. The shop occupied all the front of the under flat, and had two big windows looking to the street. A vennel or pend found its way between our landlord's house and ours, in which there was a door that led to the upper flat of the latter. There was also a door to the back leading into the back-shop, or the room behind the shop. At the back were two cellars, a washing house, the studio, and a henhouse under erection. There was also a middle-sized garden, at the bottom of which was a door opening on a footpath that lead to the sea-side.

The henhouse that my father had been erecting was now finished, and we had got a couple of hens and a cock to start with. The fowls from the day we got them until they were put away (which wasn't for years after this) were always a source of the greatest interest and amusement to me. We soon got an addition to their number, and I spent many an hour watching the fiercely contested fights the ones we had got first had with the new-comers. Before long, to my sore grief, one of the former took ill and died. Its burial was left to me; and well do I mind of digging a hole in the garden, laying some clean straw therein on which I laid the stiffened hen, with a sad heart covering it over with some more straw, and then replacing the mools on the grave of my old friend. I wasn't heeding, however, about it lying there altogether forgotten; so I got a bit smooth wood on which I printed with a lead pencil, before placing it at the head of the grave, this rather unpoetical inscription -

"Here Lies
A Poor Old Hen
Which Died
12 September 1869"

Many people got a hearty laugh, I'll warrant, at the odd epitaph, and the odder creature to whose memory it was inscribed.

About this time, Aberlady was first accommodated with gas. A few lamps, some six or seven, were put up here and there through the village which was to us youngsters was a great advantage - enabling us to play at marbles etc. on the darkest of nights, but was a great disadvantage in another, as the following incident will show. As I was returning home from some errand I had been delivering, I was met, and teased, and nicknamed to an unlimited extent by a laddie with whom I had lately had a trifling cast-out, and, as a common resource at that time among us, I lifted a stone and threw it at him; but, alas, in its flight it went clean through one of the new lamps, smashing it to a thousand pieces! Fancy with what horror I heard the crash, and with what fear I glided into the house, never speaking a word about what had happened, of course. Nevertheless, my father soon heard of the mischief I had done, and gave me due hearing about the same.

I was sitting in the back-shop pondering over what an amount of vexation a small mistake is capable of making, when I saw through the window that looked into the shop the visage of a personage alike feared and hated by all us wild laddies - in fact none other than that of the much dreaded "bobby". He spoke a wee while with my father who was in the shop; then, woe me! - I had often quailed with fear below the wrathful eye of the schoolmaster, but never was I so feared as when I heard my father's voice cry, "Come here, Johnnie!" My first thought was to run out of the house as fast as my legs could carry me, but fear had so overcome me that I felt as if I would have failed to be away in time. Just then, my father entered the back-shop saying, "Come awa', Johnnie, here's a gentleman wanting tae see ye." "Guidness pity me!" I thought as I reluctantly followed my father into the presence of the blue-coated laddie-frighter. Soon followed the inquest.

"You are John Reid, I suppose, and it was you that broke that street lamp today? Asked Mr Policeman.

No reply.

"Come speak oot the truth", said my father.

"Again I say, it was you that broke the lamp?" queried the bobby.

"Ay!" I said at last.

"Well, how was it that ye broke it?"

"It was Pate Broon aye teasin' me and ca'in' me "Reidie, peedie", that made me lift the stane an'.."

"Ou, ay!" broke in the blue-coat, "stanes again, of course; we must really put a stop to this throwin' o' stanes." Then, with a wink to my father, he added, "Now your father is scarcely willin' tae pay (as must be done for this lamp) for the issues

12

o' a' your mischievous pranks, so we think the only way to tame you a bit, is to put you in Haddington jail for a time; meanwhile, however, we'll see how you behave yourself, and don't let me catch you throwing stanes again."

"No' if I can help it", I thought to myself.

He then took his leave after a word or two with my father, and I went into the house right uneasy about the jail, yet with a sigh of relief that I was meantime out of the way of the police officer. But, as days passed, I soon found out that it had all been a device on the part of my father and the bobby to try and make me a wee thing more cautious in future, and it did succeed for a wee while, though before long I was just as hairum skairum as ever.

It was on the 20th day of October of this year (1869), that a memorable event happened near Aberlady - the stranding of a monster whale. At night, news came to the village, that, while some workers were busy lifting potatoes in a field by the sea-side, at, or near a place called Bogle Hill, a tremendous fish was seen by them to wallow in the bay in seeming distress. One of their number, a youth, instantly ran into the sea waist-deep and plunged his fork into the whale's side, at which, it is said and believed, it gave a great roar, a most unwanted act, I suppose, for such an animal. Two men afterwards shot the poor beast, which would probably have died at any rate. The news, of course, soon spread throughout the place; and next day all the scholars got away from the school after dinner-time to see the great whale. Half walking and half running, in droves we soon approached the Gosford Lodge, where we could get a complete view of the bay.

I can tell you we didn't need to look long or very minutely to see the object that we had got the play to see; although a few of us could scarcely believe that what appeared a little mountain with folk on it was, in reality, an animal, or fish rather. Aye, there were folk on it, and some standing in its very mouth! It was lying in a pool of blood, and was in length, if I mind right, about 85 feet, and of even greater proportional girth round the body. I cut, as did many others, a piece of whalebone out its immense mouth, which I still keep in memory of that day. My father took some negatives of the whale that were rather a success. in two or three days the smell of it got almost unbearable; but it was soon tugged by a steam-boat to Leith or some other place, where, I'll warrant, it would yield a good quantity of oil.

13

Chapter VII

I should have mentioned in a previous chapter that my two elder sisters Chrisie and Mary had gone to the city of Edinburgh to reside, and eke out a living at one thing and another. They had left Aberlady some time before we flitted from Diggity, as our former house was called. Also about this time, or shortly after it, my youngest sister, Maggie, left Aberlady, for Linlithgow; so that our household was reduced by that number, although we had a servant lass for some time then.

A time was now fast approaching; to which all us youngsters looked forward to with great glee: this was Christmas. The winter time had many charms to us, as well as the summer, and a shower of snow was generally hailed by us with hearty cheering. And when night there was an appearance of frost we used to dam up the gutters and fill them with water, so that if the frost should continue till morning, we would then have a fine slide, or skid as we called it. We had various ways of checking if the ice was good or not - one was to lay a knife or a bit of 'skeelie' on it, and placing a bonnet over it for a wee while, so that when the bonnet was removed and the knife or "skeelie" lifted, should the mark of whatever was placed there be impressed on the ice, we then concluded it was good ice and, if not, that it was, of course, not good. And then although we couldn't –

> "run aboot the braes,
> An' pu' the gowans fine,"

> nor

> "paddle in the burn
> Frae mornin' sun till dine,"

Yet, when it came, a fall of snow, we used to happily roll ourselves about in it, as if it were a bed of flowers; and many a rare battle we had with snow-balls - so many on each side. If the snow should cover our skids so deep that we couldn't very well clear it off with our bonnets, we used to stamp the snow hard, and then skid on it until it became a sliddery substance something like ice. As this was generally done on the foot-path, it was very much to the chagrin of the bobby, and many old folk who couldn't walk on it without the danger of getting a very hard bang, or strain in their stiffened muscles. In such like employment passed away most of our leisure hours as Christmas approached.

On Christmas eve, when the school closed at four o'clock, the cheers of the scholars might have been heard a mile and more from the village, as we then got the 'play' till after New Year's day - a whole week of glorious liberty. Not only was it a week of liberty from our task, but a week of almost continuous enjoyable events to the laddies and lassies about the place. On Christmas Day a sermon was preached to the young in the Established Kirk, when by the generosity of Mr Tait, the minister of that time, each who attended was presented with a little book or picture, an orange, a bun, and a penny, all much thought of by us youngsters.

But a far greater event was to follow. By the kind and thoughtful co-operation of some members of the Hope family of Luffness, the above mentioned minister, and a few other big folk about the place, a Christmas Tree was erected in the school, from which every laddie and lassie under fifteen years of age residing in the parish were given a ticket to draw a prize. The preparations and decorations of the school and its surroundings for the great event generally took a few days. The forms and benches had all to be taken out of the school and put in the playground, which is a bit to the back of the school. A cartful of evergreens was brought by permission from the Gosford grounds, along with the stately fir that was to represent the Christmas Tree. Some joiners were employed to decorate the school etc., and in a wee while we might scarcely know it as the place where we were, so recently, brooding over letters and figures and fearing to lift or turn our head lest we should catch the wary eye of the school-master. At length, the night came when we had to draw our prizes, or, to use a perhaps more proper term, presents. Long before the appointed time, the bairns began to congregate around the school gate, in some cases clamouring and fighting to get nearest the entrance.

All around the school, as well as within, was gaily decorated and illuminated. An arch was neatly and tastefully erected over the gate, on the top of which in big and emblazoned letters shone the word "Welcome". At the front end of the school stood the band of the village volunteers who, under the leadership of the drill instructor, Sergeant Crighton, played a selection of music that was much appreciated by the village folk in general. The gate was now opened and the bairns began to flood into the school, not with that reluctant step with which they usually entered, but with hearts fluttered with expectation, and full of happiness and joy. One half of the school had been left clear for the youngsters. in the centre of the other half was placed the Christmas Tree, and underneath it the load of various toys, wax candles etc. At the other end of the school was a small figure representing Father Christmas, with his umbrella. At the other end some gas tubes were placed in the form of the Prince of Wales' feathers which, as now seen brightly lighted up, were looked upon as an especial wonder to us easily diverted bairns. Our prizes (consisting of books, toys, knives, and such articles of clothing as bonnets, shawls, leggings, and various other useful articles) almost filled up the remainder of that half of the school. Wreaths of evergreens, such as holly of its various kinds, green an' variegated bay, yew, cyprus, juniper, ivy, and some sprigs of mistletoe, along with a variety of little pennons, mottoes, etc., in great profusion adorned the walls. The last of the youngsters now entered, the entertainment was begun by the bairns singing under the direction of Mrs Douglas Hope, who took a very prominent part in the proceedings, a kind of Christmas chant commencing -

"Good King Wenceslas look'd out
On a Christmas even',
When the snow lay round about
Deep, and crisp, and even."

The tune to which it was sung had even less to commend it than the words; nevertheless, it quite pleased us bairns, and was easily sung, and these, I presume, were the ends for which it was chosen. The next item was a magic lantern exhibition that amused all present very much indeed. Then the bairns would again sing, perhaps, "The Campbells are Comin'", or "The Boatie Rows". After a few of the leading persons had spoken and cheers given for the organisers, and "Auld Lang Syne" sung, each child was presented with their prize as they left the school, quite delighted with the few hours enjoyment.

Chapter VIII

Close following the Christmas Tree was another extraordinary night - Hogmanay, that is the last night of the year. It was extraordinary in this respect, that the majority of the laddies, as well as the lassies, about the village went guising. As night crept on, the darkness begun to grow deeper, and the shop all lighted up, I quietly slipped in behind the counter to watch the several guisers, that were likely to make their appearance in the shop very soon. When they did enter, I beheld their queer, and in some cases ghost-like dressed forms with not a little fear mixed with amusement, and I was even glad when some of the fearsomest made their exit.

First came a couple with blackened faces, dressed as an old man and an old wife - they were two laddies, or two lassies, or a laddie and a lassie for what a body might know. The old man had on a chimney-hat without the crown, a bash in the side of it, and the rim half torn away; a long-tailed surtout that hung down past the wearer's knees, and the sleeves folded half way up to let his hands out; a pair of trousers with nearly as many colours as Joseph's coat; and a pair of boots that seemed to have been made very easy for his father's corny feet. He had a bundle of rags stuffed under his coat across his shoulders in imitation of a hump, and a stick in his hand on which he feigned to have resource to support his frame. The old wife had on a mutch, which had served its turn to some old friend, with a braw coloured handkerchief tied over it; a frock through the many tears of which was here and there seen a brilliantly striped petticoat, or perhaps, as the case might be, a pair of corduroy trousers. She also wore a pair of boots that seemed to have been

17

made for some rustic giant or other. Arm in arm they approached the counter and began to sing, or rather to recite in a kind of musical manner: -

"The Minstrel boy to the war is gone
In the ranks of death you'll find him;
His father's sword he has girded on,
And the wild harp slung behind him.
Land of song, said the warrior-bard,
Though all the world betrays thee,
One sword, at least, thy right shall guard,
One faithful harp shall praise thee.

"The Minstrel fell - but the foeman's chain
Could not bring his proud soul under;
The harp he loved ne'er spoke again,
For he tore its chords asunder;
And said, no chains shall sully thee,
Thou soul of love and bravery!
Thine songs were made for the pure and free,
They shall never sound in slavery".

When finished, my father proffered the minstrels a bawbee each, but the old wife handed her's to the old man, as it was a rule among the guisers who went in such couples, or wherever there was an old man represented, that he should have charge of the silver. As they thought their song had been appreciated they again begun: -

"Old King Cole was a merry old soul,
An' a merry old soul was he," etc.

That couple had scarcely departed when in comes another guiser with his physiognomy eclipsed by a hideous false-face and a big Balmoral bonnet on his crown. He wore a great long white sark that covered him all over except the head, and the usual big boots. Gosh! The sight of this one, although just some school cronie or other, likely, made me glide close in behind my father. Giving a firm dump on the floor with his stick (which the guisers seldom went without) and placing himself opposite my father an' me, he began: -

"Was ever old warrior of suffering so weary?
Was ever the wild beast so bayed in his den?
The Southron bloodhounds lie in kennel so near me,
That death would be welcome to Callum O'Glen.

18

"My sons are all slain, and my daughters have left me,
No child to protect me where once I had ten;
My chief they have slain, and of stay have bereft me,
And woe to the grey hairs of Callum O'Glen.

"The homes of my kinsmen are blazing to Heaven,
The bright sun of morning has blush'd at the view;
The moon has stood still on the verge of the even,
To wipe from her pale cheek the tilt of the dew.
For the dew it lies red on the vales of Lochaber,
It sprinkles the cot and it flows in the pen;
The pride of the country has fallen forever,
O death! Hast thou no shaft for Callum O'Glen.

"The sun in his glory has looked on our sorrow,
The stars have wept blood over hamlet and lea;
O is there no day-spring for Scotland?
Of bright renovation for souls of the free?
Yes! One above all has beheld our devotion,
Our valour and faith are not hid from his ken;
The day is abiding, of stern retribution,
On all the proud foemen of Callum O'Glen."

"Very guid, very guid!" said my father when the song was finished, "Can yae sing ony mair?"

The white Sark replied by resuming in the same patriotic tone:-

"Gae, bring my good old harp ance more,
    Gae bring it free and fast,
For I maun sing anither sang
    Ere a' my glee be past;
And trow ye, as I sing, my lads,
    The burden o't shall be –
Auld Scotland's howes,
    an' Scotland's knowes,
An' Scotland's hills for me;
I'll drink a cup tae Scotland yet,
    Wi' a' the honours three."

Having got through his second song in a very creditable way, my father gave him a small compensation for his trouble, which he thankfully received, and went away

20

to try his fortune elsewhere. Next came into the shop three laddies, two dressed as young warriors with wooden swords by their side, and the third as a doctor. First juvenile warrior steps forward and says: -

> "Here comes in Galatian,
> Galatian is my name;
> My sword and pistol by my side,
> I hope I'll win the game."

Second juvenile warrior confronts him and answers: -

> "The game, sir, the game, sir,
> Is not into your power;
> I'll slash you, and slay you
> In less than half an hour!"

> "You, sir?"
> "I, sir!"
> "Take your sword and try, sir!"

Then each draws his sword and the fight commences. in a short time, one of the combatants falls, and the doctor is called for. That personage finds that the vanquished is not mortally wounded, and after a little operation is on his feet again, when the three are ready to depart, and only wait on their donation.

Lastly comes in a band of perhaps four or five, with their faces blackened, and a dressed in different guises; with a grin to one another they begin to sing, all in different keys, or maybe just singing as the bit of the song comes into their minds:

> "The Standard on the Braes o' Mar
> Is up an' streamin' rarely;
> The gatherin' pipe on Lochnagar
> Is soundin' loud an' clearly;
> The Hieland men,
> Frae hill and glen,
> Wi' kilted plaids,
> An' glit'rin' blades,
> An' bonnets blue,
> An' hearts sae true,
> Are coming late an' early."

They also had to get a small compensation for their song, after which they left the shop with a clamouring noise and glee. Such were some of the guisers' songs and visits to the shop in 'bygane days'.

Chapter IX

One Sabbath morning while the breakfast was getting ready down-stairs, I decided to take a tour up the stair and see if there wasn't anything that I could divert myself with. I went straight to the parlour and there saw that the grate had been taken out of its place and put nearly in the centre of the floor, for some reason I couldn't guess, nor did I care. It happened to be quite filled with shavings, sticks and coals, all ready for kindling. Now, this, I thought, was a rare chance for me to have a bit fire, so I began to look for some matches, which I got in the next bedroom; and as there was no appearance of anybody coming, I lighted one and applied it to the dry shavings. Of course, it kindled up in a clap, and for a short time I stood admiring my little achievement. Nevertheless, I soon saw that the room was getting filled with smoke, so in fear and excitement I made a few frantic attempts to put out the fire I had so thoughtlessly kindled. But these attempts proved unsuccessful, so I glided down the stair as quietly as I could, and when I had reached the bottom and was standing wondering what to do, my mother just happened to come to make me aware of the breakfast being ready.

"Mither! Mither!" I exclaimed, with a real look of terror and a feigned look of amazement, "there's shurely an awfu' reek up the stair?" Confounded, my mother saw it was really the case, and - could you expect anything else?- became quite excited over the head of it.

"Oh! Oh! Johnny, what's this? Some o' your work, eh? Tell yer faither, quick." So saying she hurried up the stair whither I followed, as I was in fact over frightened to tell my father anything about it. By this time, the smoke was so dense that my mother could scarcely find her way to the parlour where she saw it was coming from. She soon saw what was what.

"Well, well!" she ejaculated, "here's a fine pliskie ye've played this mornin', an' it Sunday tae. Open the windaes, open the windaes!"

I willingly did as I was asked, and meanwhile my mother succeeded in putting out the fire, so that the smoke now gradually went away, and we both went down the stair to our breakfast. After confessing I had kindled the fire, my mother gave me some words of warning and admonition, but that was about it as my father didn't know of my prank till some time after.

When a young laddie I was sorely subject to headaches, these, however, were very often made by myself to appear far worse than they really were, to serve a purpose of my own, which can soon be explained. I have said already, if not here, elsewhere, that I had always a great dislike to the school - I liked far better to romp and to play than to sit in the school at my books any day. And, not only did I like better to romp and play, but, in sooth, I would rather have done any mortal thing than go to the abominable school. Oftener than once - oh, I shouldn't like to say how often - when I felt the least touch of headache in the morning, I used to try and make myself as white and sickly looking as possible, and with a face as long as a leap year, I would tell my mother I didn't feel well at all. "Weel then", my over indulgent mother would say, seeing I was really not looking my usual, "gin that be the case ye will e'en hae tae get a dose o' medicine, and bide at hame frae the schule."

Obviously, a dose of salts and sinny, or Gregory's Mixture, or caster oil was anything but a pleasing prospect, but then how jolly it would be did I not need to go to the school. Gregory's Mixture was the usual dose, and as soon I had got it I listened anxiously for 'the clink o' the auld schule bell'; as soon as the last jingle died on the air I felt a thrill of joy, forsooth, that that day I was exempt from my school lessons, and I began to wonder how the master and my cronies would look when it was discovered I was absent. A safe time after the school was in, I soon revived from my exaggerated illness, and sought leave to the health giving fresher air. My parents thinking this fit, didn't hinder me from getting the desired fresher air, but warned me sternly not to go outside the garden, and said I might let the hens into the garden and watch that they didn't destroy anything, which was a delightful job for me. in such a way I spent the day, and at night I pleaded sore to win out to play with my cronies, but this wasn't granted. Next day, I would usually try the same dodge but when I saw it wasn't likely to succeed, oh, wow me! What a thought it was to me that I had once more to trudge off to the school; and pity me if any of my schoolmates told the master I had been seen out-by the previous day.

In Aberlady, and most places round about, the majority of the inhabitants used to keep a sow. And when the time came that grumphie had to be killed, it was always an exceptional day among the laddies whose father or friends it belonged to. As we never kept that 'chieftain o' the trenching crew', I was often invited by my cronies when grumphie's last day had arrived to come and see it killed. This was no great temptation to me and I seldom went. Although the laddies generally rejoiced when that event was to happen, I have also seen them crying to think that the sow, whose cruive (pen or sty) they had kept clean, as clean as possible that is, and whom they had fed since it was little bigger than a poodle dog, was at last doomed to a horrible death. One day, however, when the school came out at four o'clock Peter Black says to me:

"I say, Jock, d'ye ken big Wallace (being the name of their sow) is tae be killed the nicht?"

"The nicht, is't? Troth, an' ye'll be getting' black puddin's an' white the morn Pate!" I exclaimed.

"Ay! - I'm tae keep the bluid when he's killed, an' fegs, I'll steer it weel; sae we'll hae some rare bluidy puddin's, as you say. Man! Are you no' comin' ower tae see it? Wallace, I'll wad a saxpence, is the biggest soo in Aberlady (wi' the exception o' the schulemaister); it's mair than twenty stanes I heard my faither say. Are ye comin' ower?"

"Och! What's the guid? I want a game at Charlie ower the Water, Swim Paddy Swim, Leap-frog, Hounds an' the Tod, or something."

"Get awa', man! Ye can play at thae ony nicht – no' ilka nicht ye hae the chance o' seein' a muckle soo killed. Are ye comin'?"

"Weel, weel, what time?"

"Six o'clock."

"A' richt."

So I complied for once to go and witness the last minutes of a luckless brute. Six o'clock came, and saw many laddies, myself among them, gathered round the unconscious Wallace's sty. There was a high dyke not far from the sty, on the top of which I planted myself stride-legs, as I thought I would be quite safe there, for I wasn't void of fear altogether; and such a scene I liked best to "view from afar". I will go no further to describe the horrible scene which followed: suffice it to say Wallace didn't quit life without letting most of the village know by his hideous roars.

Chapter X

Among other recreations for the summer time that the young laddies of Aberlady have advantage of, is one that is generally very popular among both old and young - namely fishing. We laddies seldom used a rod or a line for that purpose, however; and we deemed our own way of fishing far more successful and it is extremely simple too, and good exercise into the bargain. Each Saturday, and often at night through the week, we often set off in jovial bands for the fishing, with no instrument for the occasion whatever, and only a piece of string in our pouch on

24

which to string the fish we succeeded in catching. When the tide has turned it comes slowly up the burn, which it gradually widens and deepens, and generally brings with it a number of flounders; so that was the time we chose for our fishing excursions. When we got past Kilspindie, or the Fishers' House rather, we used to pull up our trousers and sleeves as far as possible and enter the burn, elate, walking the places where the bottom was fine and sandy. With slow, short, and cautious steps we waded up against the flowing tide, never lifting the one foot by the other until we were sure there wasn't a flook below it, for all know it is the custom of that species of fish to lie flat on the sand, and this was our simple way of catching them. Although we were often cheated, we generally knew when there was a flook under our feet, where we held it firm, and reaching down a hand gripped it with thumb and fore-finger by the gills and brought it a prisoner to the surface: if it was a decent sized one, of course we kept it; but if not, we let it away again into the water. I've seen my cronies - for I myself was never a very successful fisher - go home after an hour or two fishing with a heavy string of flooks all caught in this manner. I say I was never a successful fisher? Nevertheless, I am about to relate an exceptional case in which I considered myself extremely successful.

One bonnie summer Saturday I set off in the direction of Luffness to try my luck at fishing once more. This was the very opposite direction we generally went on those fishing excursions; and more than that, which was as unwanted, on this occasion I was my leeful lone. I had gone a short distance beyond the old wooden brig which spanned the burn or the bay rather, and which is now supplanted by a new one, when, buckling up my knickerbockers, I entered the water and began to wade about in search of fish. I daresay I hadn't waded over five minutes when I succeeded in catching a braw bonnie eel - gosh, it was, I'm sure, three feet long if an inch, and as thick as my arm; and more nor that, it was - a dead one. After eyeing it admiringly from head to tail, I thought I had got quite plenty for one day's fishing; so, without thinking on the slimy skin of the beast, I swung it triumphantly over my shoulder and took the road for home. Ten minutes, or perhaps less, between running and walking, brought me to the village and another minute to our own house, little thinking how soon my pride was doomed to get a fall. I went through the vennel and just met my father at the back door.

"What's this noo? What's this noo?" he exclaimed. "Jist look, look what a mess ye've made o' yer jacket, ye careless brat! It's a funny thing ye can never keep yer claithes daicent."

This is what I had never thought of, my jacket being all slime over the shoulders and down the back; and just as my father was about to give me a licking for it, I said "But look, faither, see what a braw eel."

"Where gat ye that?" he readily inquired, and added, having an inkling of my fishing abilities, "Ye didna catch it, I'm certain."

"Yes, father," said I, "I catched it roon' at Luffness, near the timmer brig, only it was deid."

"Ha, ha, ha! Oh aye, then run awa' and put it whaur ye got it, it'll ne'er come alive oot o' the water."

"I'll gang an' let my mither see't" said I, rather crest-fallen, but hoping I would get some praise for my success in that direction. I told her all about it, and desired her to cook it, but she refused to comply, and told me to put it in the midden; my father entering, seconded the motion, all because the poor eel was dead when I caught it. Sorely disheartened I went to do my parents' bidding; and after a last long look at my prized fish, I committed it to the ashes for good and all. After returning to the house I got a good hearing about making such a mess of my jacket, for after that I couldn't wear it, except when I was doing any wee bit job about the back door or garden.

Chapter XI

It was a fine summer morning when I, having spent all the previous night playing at bools, etc., and having neglected my lessons altogether, felt more than usually averse to trudge off to the school. The bell had begun to ring and hardly a lesson could I say, so that I knew over well the punishment that was inevitable should I appear in my class, and my turn came to show my unwritten exercise, or repeat my grammar and whatever else should have been learnt. And yet, where was there a retreat or a remedy? Would I just need to take my palmies? I turned over in my 'harran-pan' all the excuses I had tried before, but none seemed to be practicable in the present case. Feigning a headache had become over stale, and over often seen through, to use a common phrase, it was 'a cock that wouldna ficht'; and neither of the other pleas seeming likely to work any more than it, I resolved in despair to openly play the fugitive and truant. So, taking my slate and books in my hands, I sneaked out at the back-door and hid them below the studio floor, there being a space of about six inches between it and the ground, as it rested on four legs, as it were, one at each corner. That done, I stole down the garden, watching that nobody saw me, and out at the door mentioned previously, whence I made my way to the sea-side. I didn't stay long there, however, as that was an over likely place to be discovered. Westward along the green I went, over the stile, up through the Kirk Park, and reached the stile at the head of the town just as the last jingle of the bell was dying in the air. As everything seemed quite, I crossed the road

26

"Whiles glowerin' roond wi' prudent cares,
Lest some ane catch'd me unawares"

and went up a seldom frequented road called "the Muir". Here I spent most of the day, looking for wild strawberries, throwing stones at any passing bird or rabbit, climbing up a tree to win at a bird's nest and gliding into a neighbouring field for a carrot or bawgie (Swedish turnip) before sitting down in some thick part of the wood to peel and eat it.

When the scholars dispersed at dinner-time, I saw one of my class chums, who informed me that, when the master was made aware of my absence, he sent a laddie over to the shop to inquire the reason for me being absent, who returned with the news that neither father nor any of the others had known I wasn't at the school, as I had left the house with my books and slate when the bell rung at nine o'clock. Then my schoolmate, after describing how they had got on with their lessons, etc., asked me, as was quite natural, what I had been doing with myself all forenoon, and lauded my pluck for playing truant; but concluded, however, with observing that he wouldn't like to be me to have to face the schoolmaster the following day.

Before the school went in again at one o'clock, I chanced to see another of my schoolmates, this was Jack Heriot - Jack Heriot do I say? - Aye! Jack Heriot, my old cronie! What recollections does the sound of thy name bring to my mind; but, ah, they are all dulled with sorrow and regret when I think of the flowers of three summers and the snows of three winters have fallen on thy lovely bed! - Well, this Jack Heriot, who is now taking his long rest, also asked me what I had been doing all forenoon, and why I hadn't gone to the school, and was quite fascinated with the description - exaggerated no doubt - I gave him of my running away, and my explorations throughout the forenoon. But it soon struck him that I must be hungry and, although I tried to convince him to the contrary, he ran down into the house, and soon returned with a big 'faurl of peasemeal-bonnie' which I relished. Almost immediately after this, the school bell began to ring, which I listened to with very mixed feelings; and as I ventured to look down the village, I saw all my mates running helter-skelter for the playground, from whence they had to march into the school, some pocketing their bools, some knocking the dirt off the knees of their trousers which had gathered there during that game, some shoving their peeries and string into their pockets, and some slyly glancing into their books to keep in mind their lessons. I spent the afternoon with a laddie who had been kept at home from the school to 'keep the hoose', which, however, he didn't do very well, as he and I were playing in the back-garden mostly all the time.

At night, a good while after the school had closed for the day, I ventured into the very heart of the village, and there played with my cronies at sundry games. I had

27

resolved not to enter the house that night, and had made plans on how I'd spend it, intending to steal into the hay-loft at the back of Simpson's house when all was quite, and there rest my weary bones till day-break. Nevertheless, it chanced to be as I was enjoying myself at the game of 'Change a Sixpence', that I saw my cousin Maggie coming up the village; and as she neared and came straight to myself, I was about to show a clean pair of heels, when she said something that arrested me, and I turned to speak with her. She had come, she said, to tell me that my father was at that time out somewhere, and if I came into the house now, I might get away to my bed without a licking. At first I felt inclined to refuse this offer, but at a second thought I deemed it prudent to take the chance afforded; so I went into the house, and after eating a "piece", I glided right thankfully away to bed. As it was rather late when my father came in, and I was soon asleep, he desisted from chastising me that night, but resolved to let me hear about it in the morning.

In the morning, as soon as I awoke, I put on my clothes and glided quietly out of the house, intending to have another day's sport and freedom, as I considered it. Before school time, however, with over much self confidence I ventured too near the shop, as my father saw me, and out after me as hard as his, at that time, not very robust, health would permit. I didn't think twice on what to do, but ran up the village as if for life, and was just entering the gate of Brown's joiner shop when my father caught me. A sorry and downcast prisoner, he took me by the collar of my jacket down to the house, where, despite the entreaties of my indulgent mother, I got the soundest thrashing I ever got in my life; and, moreover, he took me over to the school, which was just going in at the time, where I expected to get another licking, which to my great astonishment, but not sorrow, I didn't get. This, I think, was the last time I openly played truant.

Chapter XII

One Friday afternoon, not long before the school came out, after giving a sly glimpse around to convince me the master wasn't looking, I said to Sandy Sinclair, who was sitting next to me in the desk:

"I say, Sandy, man, I want tae get a string o' birds' eggs. Will ye come an' help me look for some the morn?"

The reply was ready. "Aye, well I ken o' a blackie an' a hempie up the loan. Shot, shot!" he whispered as the master's foot was heard approaching, which, however, soon retreated again, when he resumed. "And I ken o' another twa or three birds that were biggin' an' should hae eggs by this time. Weel, what time will we start?"

"Och, ony time ye like," I answered, "say aboot nine o'clock?"

28

"A' richt. I'll be up at the Cross at nine."

Next morning, after having transported a good plateful of porridge and sweet milk into my stomach, and with 'a shining morning face', I set out to see if my cronie had yet arrived at our meeting place - the Cross. The Cross, which I think I have not before described, or even mentioned, is a plain but ancient structure in the middle of the village on the northern side of the street. It will measure, I daresay, about ten feet square at the base, with three steps, and then a square block, on which stands a square pillar, the whole being about twelve feet high. This being quite near the school is, or used to be at any rate, the general rendezvous of the scholars; here the lassies played at chucks, etc., though probably not left in peace to do so; and it was always a great feat among the laddies to climb up the pillar and stand with one foot on the top of it.

Well I went to the Cross but, being early, saw nothing of my expected cronie; so I sat down on one of the steps to await his arrival. Aberlady was now just looking its best; the unclouded sun of that bright May morning was shedding its rays all over the fresh, clean, and quiet village; high in the air a lark, unseen but not unheard, was trilling forth his long and varied song; upon a bonnie flourishing hawthorn a mavis was ringing out his richly-toned melody; while the sparrows among the newly clad trees were adding their cheerful though humble chirrup to the chorus of Nature. But now I espied two laddies coming from the east end of the village; one was Sandy Sinclair and the other Bob Murray, another schoolmate and a renowned bird-nestler.

"Hulloh! Bob!" says I, "are ye gaun tae?"

"Aye!" said Sandy Sinclair, "we wad ne'er hae ony luck gin Bob Murray was'na wi' us."

So the three of us set off on our bird-nestling expedition. We started with the wood at the west end of the village, where we found several nests; but they were all empty except a Blackie's with three young, which we left alone. Emerging from the wood, if the little clump of trees may be dignified by the name, we proceeded round "the Muir", carefully searching the hedge on each side of the road.

"What's that?" I queried as I saw Sandy lifting his hand into the hedge on the opposite side.

"A Hempie", was the reply.

"What has it?" was the next question

29

"Haud on! - three, four - aye, four", and he brought the four little blue eggs out to our view.

"There's nae use takin' them a'", said I, as I knew my cronies were not heeding much about eggs themselves. "Twa'll dae me fine."

"That wad be daein' nae guid", returned Sandy. "E'en tho' ye only ta'en ane, the bird wadna come back again tae its nest, except they're black-sittin' (half-hatched)."

So the four eggs were blown: I presume that process is just over well known - a wee hole is made with a pin in the small end, and a rather bigger hole in the thicker end, when the contents are blown out by putting the mouth to the small end. I got two, and Bob and Sandy one apiece. We deemed the safest way to carry the eggs was to put them inside our bonnets on our heads, which we did.

"I ken o' a Blackie aboot here" said Bob Murray, as we resumed our search. "It had twa eggs a while sin' - oh, here it is! Saftly noo, saftly; she's on! Ah, there she's aff". So saying he thrust his hand into the hedge, and brought out five eggs, which were quite warm.

"I wad bet sixpence they're black-sittin'!" exclaimed Sandy Sinclair.

"They're shure tae be", I agreed.

But Bob wouldn't be convinced, and would try one. His attempt to blaw it, however, was in vain; and at length he broke it, when a young bird was seen in a pretty advanced stage of development. The other four eggs were put back again into the nest.

"What hae ye there?" asked my cronies when they saw me make an attempt to get at a nest in a thick part of the hedge.

"Anither Blackie, I think; na, it's a Mavis", I replied as I felt the hard lining of clay and dung o' the nest.

"Wi' hoo many?"

"Three, here they are. Eh, there's ane broken; they're fresh eneuch at ony rate!"

So after the Mavis' eggs were blown, I put them beside the Hempie's. We had gone along a bit without finding any more nests, when Bob stopped all of a sudden.

31

"I ken o' a Bully (Bullfinch) in this thorn tree; see, yonder it is. Gie's a dookie up. There noo, canny! Och, fient a thing has it"

And so we again proceeded, rather disappointed at the bully, which is a very uncommon bird in that quarter. A wee bit further along we discovered another hempie's nest; it had five young, which, as we moved the twigs above their nest, opened their red-lined gabs to a wonderful extent, thinking I suppose, it was their mother with some meat for them. Soon after this we entered the Whinnie Wood, which has derived its name, I gather, from the number of whin bushes it contains. Here we separated ourselves a wee bit, Bob taking as his part, the hedge, while Sandy and I went more into the interior of the wood. Before we had gone many yards I had occasion to draw my chums' attention to a nest in a whin bush, saying:

"Here's a nest with three eggs, - confound thae jags!"

"An' confound thir jags!" echoed Sandy as he tumbled over a bramble bush.

"But what is't?" asked Bob.

"I'm no' shure," I returned, "I think it's a Green Lintie. Aye, it is; red an' black spots, aye, aye!"

As one broke in the blowing, the remaining two were put beside the rest in the crown of my bonnet. Scarcely had we resumed our respective places when Sandy's voice was heard.

"Come here! Come here! Here's anither my lads!"

"What?" I asked as I approached.

"A Sprug's, I guess by the look o' it, wi' five, six, na seven, by Jove!"

"Aye, just a Spurdie's," I remarked when I saw the grey speckled eggs. Sandy got three of them, Bob two, and I, two. Here Sandy's eye happened to light on something like a nest up a very high tree.

"What's yon? Geyan like a Cushie's nest, I think".

"Aye, it is." Bob and I rejoined at the same time.

"But hoo are we tae get at it?" was the next question; "we canna breast that tree, an' there's nae branches near the bottom."

32

"I'll speil it, though," said Bob resolutely, "you, Jock, as ye're the biggest, gie's a dookie up on yer shouthers, cockie-ridie-roosie. There noo, that's it. I'll dae noo."

And as he had got on to the first branch, he wasn't long in reaching the nest. Bob had grappled about the nest for some time, Sandy and I watching with eager curiosity to know what it was, when at length we asked him.

"I dinna ken richtly what it is," was his slow rejoinder, "the funniest nest e'er I saw – fient' a hole can I find in - Oh! Oh!" he roared, and but for that part of the tree being thickly beset with branches, I'm certain he'd have fallen to the ground.

"What's wrang?" we surprisingly demanded.

"Oh, the brute! Stanes, stanes! Look at it! Stane it, ye sumphs!"

We looked, and lo, a squirrel was nimbly making its way from branch to branch and from tree to tree! No stones, however, could we get, and the squirrel was soon out of sight; while Bob came cannily down the tree and showed us where the brute had bitten him. We again took our appointed places, and soon found out a mavis' nest with five eggs; but, as we had some of those eggs already we passed on without harrying it. As Bob was making endeavours to get at a nest in the hedge, Sandy and I went over to ascertain what it was.

"It's a Katie Wran's" said he, "but the hole's i' the other side. I'll win at it enoo, though;" and he scrambled through the hedge.

"Put in yer twa fingers, canny, Bob, an' see what it has," said my other cronie advisedly.

"The wee barley pickles! I cannae count them; they're cauld tho', sae nae winna be black-sittin'. See, there's twa or I get the lave."

"Ah! Dinna harry it", said I, "min' the auld proverb –

> "Thus saith Robin Redbreast,
> And the Jenny Wren –
> "If you harry my nest,
> You'll never grow tae men"."

"Grow tae men?" echoed Bob, "what's aboot it man; are we no' far better as we are?" And I won't say other than that he was right on that point. We soon discovered it had six eggs, two of which we got each.

"There's a nest alang there a bit," I observed; and Bob was off like a shot to see what it was.

"A Mavis full bug, or else harried or forsaken; and here's anither just biggin' - a Hempie's, I think."

"And here's a Shifta up here," put in Sandy, as he made his way up a stunted elm tree. He was soon at the nest and informed us it had four eggs, which he was for bringing down in the nest, it was so neat, he said; but I entreated him to let the nest be, which he reluctantly did, adding, it would do no good there, tho' it was the neatest nest he'd ever seen, no bird would ever come to it again.

"Dinna be sae shre aboot that," I returned, "That jist puts me in min' o' a bit story aboot a bird's nest, that I'll tell ye as I heard it, and I believe it tae be fact. Weel! D'ye ken that big hoose wi' the ivy on't at the fit o' the Wynd? My granfaither, an' faither tae, I think, lived in it at this time. Noo there happen'd tae be swallows nestin' in ane o' the windaes, which bein' left alane, and no' dung doon, as some hard-hearted folk wad hae done, it had in its time, fowre young; an' after these were strong eneuch on the wing, a' the swallows forgaithered on the top o' the hoose, whaur they held a meetin', and finally left for a warmer clime when the October winds were divestin' the trees o' their foliage. Early neist Spring a spurdie, thinkin' it was it was a fine chance tae occupy the swallows' nest, an' thereby save her the trouble o' biggin ane for hersel', made the little hoose o' clay her hame. But, my fegs, she got a stern reward for her audacity and laziness! She had eggs, and they in due time were hatched, and were nearly fu'-feathered when the swallows returned. The former tenants o' the clay biggin', seein' their nest ta'en possession o' by the ignoble sprug, gaithered a' their kith an' kin thegither, gaed tae the ditch in a flock, each loadin' itself wi' a guid nebfu' o' clay, whence they proceeded tae the nest where the unsuspectin' spurdie was nursin' her young, and completely built up the hole! In which way they left the luckless inmates tae die o' hunger, or for want o' air."

"Three cheers for the swallows!" warmly ejaculated my cronies, as we turned in searched of more nests. In a short time we were at the eastern extremity of the Whinnie, and before going any further we resolved to have a bit rest and a crack. But I find it necessary to make another chapter of our bird-nestling adventures.

Chapter XIII

Leaving the Whinnie we passed Aberlady Mains, and along the road that leads to Luffness Mains searching the hedges on our way, of course. We saw no nests, however, until we came to a short dyke, when Bob Murray told us he knew of an

Ox-ee that was building a nest in it, about a fortnight since. Many straws were seen sticking out the hole, which seemed to verify Bob's statement. But how were we to find a way into a nest, the entrance to which wouldn't let in two fingers? Nonetheless, by means of an iron stanchel that was lying nearby, we were enabled to runch out the stone immediately below the hole. Then, after some loose bits of lime were cleared away, it was an easy matter to search the nest.

"What has it?" was our invariable interrogation, as Bob put in his han'.

"Eggs at ony rate", was the ready answer, "fowre, five, six – no, five. Here they are. What wee duffers!"

Ay, indeed, they were wee things, an' took some care in their blowing as they were turned, as we termed it - that is, between fresh and black-sitting, in the first stage of being hatched.

"Whaur will we gang noo?" I inquired of my elated cronies.

"Let's gang up the strip an' intae the Maggie's Wa's wud," suggested Bob, airtin' that way.

"No!" returned Sandy, "Let's gang intae the Draubbie Wa', an' awa' doon by Luffness; - what say ye, Jock?"

"Well!" said I, addressin' the latter, "I think yer gate's the best, an' then we'll get ower tae the links."

Although not without some trouble we obtained eggs of various bird species including Sand Martin, Fieldy (or Fieldfare), Corncraik, Woodlark, Yellow Yorlin (or Yellow Yite), Whautie, Willie Muff, Partridge, Waterhen, Peeseweep, Tubie (or Redshank) and Restrock and trudged away home quite proud of our day's work, although very weary and as hungry as hawks.

"Where hae ye been a' this time?" asked my mother as I entered the house; then, seeing me take the eggs out of my pockets answered her own question, - "Ah! I see, harrying birds' nests ye scoondrel! – What's those, paitrichs? – Eh, laddie, ye're nae feard! What if the policeman had seen ye?"

"Oh, we took care of that – but, Mither, I want thae twa paitrich eggs. We'll blaw them intae the fryin'-pan and I'll get thae waterhens an' peeseweeps some other time, if ye winna use them yersels. They're as guid as hens ony day, an' the peeseweeps a haundle sicht better. Hech! But I'm unco' hungry."

35

"Its braw tae be hungry and ken o' meat," she responded as she put my tea and dinner combined before me. After I'd eaten a hearty meal, I procured a string thread on which I began to string my eggs. In the centre I put the Partridge, a Waterhen's on each side of them, then the Peeseweep's (for I've blown them all into the pan, as my father and mother said they'd try them), then the Tubie's and the Cushie's and so on according to size until I ended with the Ox-ee's and Jenny-Wren's. In a few days, however, they got a mishap, when most of them were broken, to my unutterable grief; yet for some reason or other I never tried to get them replaced – so much the better for the bits of poor innocent birdies.

Whoever may chance to peruse these pages, may think that our bird-nesting excursion was rather too successful to be altogether true. If such is the opinion, I must say it is a just one, as I am bound to admit such a day's nestling was never undertaken or partaken in by me. Nonetheless, mostly all the incidents related therein are true, although happening on different occasions, which I have here compressed into one day's nestling, so that I may not need to broach the subject again. I have also endeavoured to mention all the commoner birds in the district, and some of the usual places they chose to build.

Chapter XIV

A chastisement, still common enough in some schools I presume, to which our Aberlady teacher had often times resource, was that of shutting up the unlucky culprit – for the laddie or lassie that couldn't say their lessons or committed the enormous crime of smiling or whispering to their mates, were, and in some schools still are, treated little better – in a little closet off the bigger school-room. As I was always among the dunces, and otherwise a careless and insubordinate pupil, and the master having, moreover, a personal prejudice against myself, maybe in consideration of these very faults, and that he generally failed to make me ashamed or 'gar me greet', I had often to spend some weary hours in that little unpopular apartment. One afternoon then, I was shut up in the closet, for what I don't well remember, and I dare say it wouldn't matter; there was very little in it, only the basin for soaping the floor, etc.; but it had a window, through which I watched the Spurdies hopping about, envying their liberty, no doubt, and shortly saw some of the younger classes pass on their way home, whom, doubtless, I likewise envied. Sick at heart when I thought of the present, but bright and hopeful when I pictured the happy future when I would no longer be under the hateful restraint of school laws, time flowed by, and I saw class after class pass the window, until, at length, my own passed, some of whom glowered in through the panes to see how I was getting on. Each minute I expected the master to enter and release me, but no-one came near me. Everyone was now out of the school, and I heard the master lock the outer door, before he ultimately went to the house, leaving everything about the school as quiet as the grave. I then wondered whether he had forgotten about me altogether, or whether he meant to try my patience, and give me my fill of a closet life. After having been fully an hour in the closet since the master left the school, I at length heard a foot-step approach the outer door, which, however, was away too slow for that of the master. At last, the door of my prison opened, and there, astounded, stood Belle Allan, the old woman who cleaned the school, etc.

Guidness! Laddie," she exclaimed, "what a fricht ye've gi'en me. What are you daein' here at this time o' day? Does the maister ken ye're here?"

"I dinna ken," I replied to her latter question, "he might."

"I'll gang an' see, then," said she, as she waddled off to the schoolhouse. In a short time the old body returned saying, "Ye've to gang awa' hame, the maister says; an' high time tae. I think he'd forgotten aboot ye, altho' he didna say't."

"Ay, is he ashamed or feard tae come an' tell me himsel'?" was my boastful rejoinder, as I gladly took leave of my place of confinement, for the meantime at any rate.

The year 1870 was near its close, and the Merry Christmas time was at hand – but, alas, it was anything but a merry Christmas to our family! My oldest sister, Chrisie, was ill with smallpox, which disease was raging in Edinburgh at that time; and my father was in town attending her sick-bed. While, at the same time, my youngest sister, Maggie, in Linlithgow, was very ill. Christmas passed, and the last day of the year had come; but, sorry day, before it closed Maggie was no more! Next day (New Year's Day of 1871), while round about was heard the greetings of friends wishing each other a Happy New Year, came the sorrowful news to our already sorrowing household that Chrisie had crossed the 'Dark Valley of the Shadow of Death', unconscious that her sister had 'gone before'. The elder of the two was just in the prime of her youth, while the younger was just approaching it.

> "Leaves have their time to fall,
> And flowers to wither at the north wind's breath,
> And stars to set; - but all,
> Thou hast all seasons for thine own,
> Oh Death!"

These were the first, I may say, of a series of family bereavements that ultimately left me very scant of near relations.

"Friend after friend departs, -
Who hath not lost a friend?
There is no union here of hearts,
That has not here an end."

The two sisters were buried in one grave at the family burying ground in Gullane
Kirkyard. O Mortality! Although the day may still be distant, it is the unavoidable
fate of us all: -

"A few days may, a few years must,
Consign us to the silent dust!"

At the Whitsunday term of the year 1872, we flitted from the house opposite the
school, in which we had lived for three years, to the one still tenanted by my
mother, and situated within a dyke and pailing at the foot of the Wynd. My father,
who, by this time, had been long in a precarious state of health, greatly augmented
by the death of Chrisie and Maggie, was now about to give up the shop altogether,
and devote his time more to photographing, when able. The house to which we
were about to flit had hitherto been a one flatted cottage, as was also that next
door; but the landlady, Mrs Reid, had added a storey and attics to it, and otherwise
fitted it up anew.

As it was ready for us some time before the term, we had the convenience of
taking down the furniture when it best suited; and, so, two or three days before
Whitsunday I had the glorious privilege of being allowed to stay away from the
school to help with the flitting. A laddie, Sandy Crawford, who had just left the
school at that time, helped me transport a lot of sundry articles down the Wynd in a
wheelbarrow, and deposit them, without any regard for order, in a great heap in the
kitchen of our new house; so that, when the term day came, there was so much, at
least, that hadn't to go down with the carts. We then took leave of the house and
shop where everything had become familiar –

"For doon the Wynd the heapit team
Swung hameward, rockin' noddin';
The household goods porteous gleam,
O' instant wreck forboding;
But ropes an' strae made guid that day
Tae haud in coalition,
Clocks, tables, stuils, beds, chairs, an' dales,
Secure – despite position."

Again it fell to my lot to flit the animate objects – the cat and the hens. The former
returned to the house we had once such a job to get her reconciled to, as often as

38

she did to Diggity, when we flitted thence. It was some time before we got settled down a bit, and things put in their proper places, after which, however, we found it a comfortable home.

Chapter XV

Across the road, a wee bit from our new house is a joiner's shop, which at this time belonged to Mr Mitchell of Harelaw, who employed a considerable number more workman than can now find employment there. We laddies often used to visit this shop (as well as the one at the other end of the clachan) for shavings, or with some message, and not very seldom with no excuse whatsoever except to see the joiners working, and get a crack and perhaps some fun with the apprentices.

One day, then, about dinner time I thought I'd go over and see what was going on in the joiner's shop, and had no sooner entered the gate than I observed two of the apprentices and a journeyman, to boot, enjoying themselves at the sawpit. This sawpit was some fifteen yards long and several feet deep, and was, at this time, filled with water, into which the joiners had launched a muckle tub to serve as a boat, in which one of the apprentices was now getting a sail while his mates were looking on and preparing for their turn. At length it was proposed and agreed that I should get a turn as well; so, with great glee I boarded the circular boat and for a short time, to my satisfaction propelled it along through the water by taking hold of the pailing that fenced the pit. The journeyman, however, proposed a better way of getting a sail, as he said; so, taking a long piece of wood by the end, he told me to hold on by the other, and he would pull me along in that way. That we did; but scarcely had the tub got into the middle of the pit, when, either by accident, or as might be possible, for he was a very tricky loon, by design, he let go the stick, round went the tub, and down went I into the dirty water, heels uppermost. in a twinkling my friends were by my side, or rather by the side of the pit opposite the spot where I was immersed, and with; their assistance I was speedily on dry land again, where I stood for a minute, wondering at the half-stunned sensation I felt, and the spectacle of my dripping clothes, which, you may be assured, was the source of much laughter to the joiner laddies.

With a good sight less glee than I had entered the joiner's yard, I made my exit, and went across the road for the house, while the water in my boots at each step was singing "splash, splash, splash!" Before coming within sight of the windows I stopped behind the dyke to meditate on what I would say to my father when I appeared in such a plight. As I deemed it would be twice as bad if he knew I had met the mishap in the sawpit, I resolved to say (for then I wasn't over particular in speaking the direct truth) I had fallen into the burn while crossing the "steps" – stones laid across the burn at very irregular distances, and of various dimensions and shapes, also being mostly covered with a green slimy sea-weed, so that it was not uncommon for the person attempting to cross them to miss his or her footing. Although that was the story I told my father, he discovered the whole truth before long.

The two principal and only general holidays in the year to the working folk of Aberlady, are the Carter's Play - the Fair - or as it is generally termed here, the Race, and Old Hansel Monday. The latter I must pass over just now, but will say something of it hereafter, and meanwhile try to describe, as shortly as possible, some of the incidents relative to the former in bygone days. When the Race originated I cannot say; but ever since I was brought to light it has been held on the last Tuesday of June. It used to be looked forward to with a good deal of interest by almost each inhabitant of the parish; and when I say that you may have an inkling that to us youngsters it really was a bright golden speck in the background of futurity. Long, long, (at least it seemed very long to us), before the time we gathered all our bawbees together and tentily kept them in our "penny-pigs", so that we could spend a few pennies on fancy articles that were not to be had in Aberlady, either for love or silks, except on the Race day. The nearer that extraordinary day approached the greater grew our expectations, till, at length, the night preceding it, when the school closed our ecstasy knew no limit. And when we went, or, rather, were sent, to our beds, the big thoughts of the morrow in our young minds kept "Willie Winkie" at defiance for a long time; and always as we tossed and turned the rhyme would force itself upon us: - "The morn's the fair, and I'll be there, etc.," until, at long and last, we fell asleep to dream of gingerbread and candy, and the sound of penny trumps.

When we got up next morning, and with fluttering hearts went over the door, we could see that the Wynd had assumed a very busy appearance, with the throng of the Edinburgh folk, who had travelled all night with their vans and arrived at our clachan at an early hour, erecting their stands in a row down the west side of the street. It was about nine o'clock in the morning, if I mind rightly, that at the house of a certain lady - old lady I was go to say, but that would be sacrilege – each laddie and lassie in the parish who went there were presented with tuppence, given by the thoughtful and generous Miss Hope of Luffness, through the agency of the above-mentioned lady, who handed it to the bairns with as much pride, consequence, condescension, grace and satisfaction, as if she was the munificent donor. Shortly after this a good number of young ploughmen, etc., mostly from the neighbouring farms of Craigielaw and Aberlady Mains, congregated in the village with their horses most extravagently dressed up with diverse coloured braids, ribbons, mirrors, and such like showy articles, from their noses to the tips of the tail, - and they themselves with a sash over their broad shoulders. The head one among them was called "My Lord", and he bore a banner on the end of a pole bearing the well-known motto, "God Speed the Plough;" – which flag, by the way,

40

was displayed on the village green last year where the games were held. Of course, to us youngsters this assemblage of men and horses was of the greatest interest, as we verily thought it about the finest sight imaginable.

The Penston brass band, always procured for the occasion, having arrived, took the lead through the village, with the prancing horses in its wake, together with a large concourse of laddies and lassies, and a few older folk to boot. They made a short tour through the surrounding district, visiting Craigielaw, Gosford, Harelaw etc., where at each place they made a short stay and danced to the spirited music of the band. When we returned from our trip with the band and horses, the stands, from the corner at the top of the Wynd to the bottom had now been completely erected, the white canvas coverings of which were glaring in the heat of the summer sun, and the braw things for sale were temptingly laid out on the tables. With what unbounded rapture we beheld that scene, and with what feelings I now see it in my memory, are far beyond my power of description.

The stands were of various sizes and of various kinds; here was one with gingerbread, here one with candy, here one where we shot for nuts, here one with toys, etc., the owner of which was bawling out "Cheap John! Cheap John! All a penny, all a penny!" Here one with sherbet, etc., etc. Now then was our time to spend our pennies, an' far over soon they slipped out our fingers as we patronised the different stands, those with the gingerbread and candy probably the most, and over often too, as was proven in some cases by a sickness or headache next day. Nor must I forget to mention, among other notables, old Geordie Borthwick with his famous "Roly Poly". I still think I see the good-natured old worthy, not that 'fu'' but just with a good drop in his eye. He is now dead a good while since, I believe.

By this time, I'll warrant, the clachan was ringing with the sound of penny whistles and other cheap little instruments, the echo of which still seems to linger in my ears. In the afternoon, about four o'clock, the band of the Aberlady Rifle Volunteers marched through the street, playing some music that was deservedly appreciated, to the village green where the games had now to take place. These athletic sports generally went off very satisfactorily, before a large gathering of spectators, who enjoyed the scene, which was kept lively and interesting by the unflagging zeal of the managers. The Games over, the band returned up the village to the Drill Hall where the prizes were distributed, while we took our last bawbees to the stands where they were soon exchanged for other things. To finish up the day's proceedings a ball was always got up in the said Hall, where "My Lord" and his "Lady" lead off the dances, which wound up at about five o'clock in the morning.

41

These few years past, Aberlady has never assumed the same stir on the Race day as in the years I have described; many of the old customs having died out. And although the events and prizes in the programme of Games (the chief attraction of the day) are still much the same, and are generally well contested, there is a perceptible want of energy in the proceedings, which augurs that even the Games may not see many more years. It is with the deepest regret I observe, and with greatest reluctance I admit, the sad truth that so many of the youths of my native village nowadays are more likely to spend their time and silver in the public houses, than in keeping up any manly sport, or any beneficial association.

Chapter XVI

I must begin this chapter by mentioning the death of my beloved father. One March morning, 1873, when getting up, I was told by a weeping relative that my father had crossed that burn whence no traveller returns. I've noted in a preceding chapter my parent's declining health; but little thought I, at least, he was really "wearin' awa' tae the land o' the Leal." I can't describe the unutterable grief I experienced that day, but, suffice to say, it was the bitterest day in my life – made doubly bitter by the thought that I had been an undutiful and unkind son. How many things now I wished I had left undone; and what kindnesses I was now willing to have shown, when too late! I felt as if, and believed at the time, I would never be happy in this life again; but, the flight of time, which works wonders, has proven it otherwise. With tear-filled eye, I followed my father's bier to Gullane Kirkyard, and saw him laid near where my two sisters had been laid not so long before.

Often since then have I thought on those days of dool, and the dear father I had lost so early and still, in fancy, I see –

> "those angel-faces smile,
> Which I have loved long since, and
> lost awhile."

To describe his many virtues in my weak sentences, wouldn't give justice to the noble sire, whose memory I revere more than anything - so shall pass from the subject.

Our new house, being quite close on the sea-green, afforded me the convenience of knowing most of what was going on there among my mates, and the opportunity of enjoying myself on that dear recreation ground whenever I liked. I gradually got fonder and fonder of daundering by the sea-shore for, even then, I seemed to be susceptible of the truth that there is:

"A rapture by the lonely shore,
Society where none intrudes,
By the sea, and music in its roar";

until almost all my leisure hours were spent on the soft, flower-spangled turf or shelly sands that edge our Aberlady Bay. In my wanderings by the sea-shore I often met a young laddie who seemed to be about as often there as myself; and, as we were schoolmates, and otherwise well-known to one another, we generally kept each other company in our adventures, and in a very short time became 'unco thick an' pack thegither'. This new cronie of mine, Jamie Bird, though I was perhaps somewhat bigger, was some months older than I, and the son of the Established Kirk precentor, who followed 'the unpoetical, yet, wherewithal honourable occupation of a teylour', or, in other words, the village tailor and precentor. The old proverb says, 'birds of a feather flock together', and, although I wasn't a bird, still Jim Bird and I were of the same wild disposition, our tastes running a good deal in the same channel; and then, 'a fellow-feeling makes us wondrous kind' so, after this for a long time, we were almost invariably seen together on the sea-shore in our hours of liberty. We now began to make some use of our wanderings, however, in as much as we gathered all the bits of wood – at least as much as we could carry – and any other thing worth the lifting that was washed in by the sea; always, if possible, going out when the tide was on the ebb.

At first our rounds were limited to within a short distance of the village, but gradually that limit was exceeded until it was our practice to go almost the length of Jova's Neuk, about 3 miles from Aberlady, and at times reaching the Neuk itself. Sometimes we went empty handed trusting to get a bit of wood we could carry on our shoulders, or some smaller pieces we could take in our arms; sometimes we took a bit of rope to tie the sticks together, or haul them along the sands, and sometimes a sheet or a bag in which to put the chips of wood, etc. we were always sure to find plenty of, though these we generally left if we could get bigger pieces. We made our rounds on the shore oftener in the winter time, for a while setting off most each night for then we were more likely to get a good find, while nobody might see us. Moreover, there wasn't so much enticement, for us, at any rate, to stay at home. Our hearts got fairly into that kind of work, and, though we didn't exactly wish for wrecks, or anything serious to befall the hardy sailors, still, it wasn't without a seasoning of delight that we beheld a passing storm, as we then had greater chance to find something worthwhile 'cast up by the sea'; for we had now become, as it were, young wreckers on a small scale. In the following chapters, I intend to relate a few of those wanderings in search of wreckage, though they may not prove very interesting, as they have a very firm grip of my memory, and, somehow or other, I like to ponder over them.

Chapter XVII

It was a Friday night about six o'clock in early winter, when Jim Bird and I set off on our tour round the sea-shore. We had an old bow bag each, and, following the example of my cronie, I bashed in one of the bottom corners of mine, until the extreme corner of one side was pressed within that of the other, and then put it over my head, the mouth of the bag reaching down my back to the calf of my leg, thus serving as hood, cape, and cloak in one. in this guise, and with our hands in our pouches, we happily stepped out along the road in the direction of the brig, indulging in prospective surmises as to what we should find, after the recent storm, when we crossed to the other side of the brig. There was a thin sprinkling of snow over the face of bleak nature, except under the sea-mark, where the snow never lies except in the severest frost; but the night was comparatively mild, and the almost full moon was already a good bit up in the heavens, and very opportunely lightening the scene of our nightly rounds.

"Isna the mune bonnie the nicht!" I remarked, when we had gone silently on a short space, both looking at that sweet silvery orb of night.

"Aye, man, aye!" he answered. "An' bricht it is, tae, ye'd maistly think ye see the Man making his shine. Noo, what think ye the lichts an' shadows on the face o't are?"

"Weel, I believe they're howes an' knowes," I replied, shortly, not knowing much about it.

"Howes and knowes? – An' what is it that mak's it gie a licht, then?"

"Ah! We've something tae learn ere we ken that, my Cock of the North! An' speakin' o' learnin'," I added, "hae ye gat ony o' yer Monday's lessons learned yet?"

"Fient a haet o' them!" he exclaimed carelessly, "But there's rowth o' time yet, man. – Hae ye gat your's learnt; ye've mair nor hiz, I suppose?"

"Aye, weel – I – what hae we! I ha'ena learned ony yet, but I think I can say my Psalm, at least as muckle o't as I'll learn – that's the third verse. Ye ken we aye gat a bit o' a Psalm tae recite on the Mondays; it's generally fowre verses we get, an' d'ye see? We get a verse tae say each, an' as I'm seventh in the class, that's the verse I'll get."

"Aye," said Birdie; "an' ye're seventh in the class, are ye?"

44

"Im-hm!" I replied like our old enemy 'as he wauchled throu' Beith'.

"An' hoo mony's in the class?" further interrogated my cronie.

"Ou, there's jist seven enoo," was my reluctant answer.

"Ay, aye! Ha, ha, ha! Sae ye'll be dooby?"

"Weel, weel, the tae end's as guid as the tither, an' a d----d sicht better, as Paddy wad say."

By this we were across the brig - not the same brig as spans the Peffer now-a-days, although at the same place, but an old structure somewhat lower than the present, and sadly in need of repair, about half a dozen spars being awanting at some places, making it difficult to get over, - and, as the tides were very low at the time, we crossed the sands a bit to win to the shore – the high-water mark of the latest tide being what we designated 'the shore'.

For some distance, after the shore was reached, there was nothing to be seen worth lifting, so, as was our practice, we commenced a-singing to cheer the way. Although our vocal powers were little better than those of a bubbly-jock, our attempts in that line quite pleased one another, and there was no other body likely to hear us, as it was a most extraordinary occurrence should we chance to see anybody in our lonely wanderings. At first we would sing alternately, and then, perhaps, together. And as the wild-ducks often flew over us, their "quack, quack, quack" was ready chorus.

"Come on, Birdie," said I, "are ye no' gaun tae gie us a song the nicht?"

"Ou, aye" he replied, "but I think ye suld sing first!"

"I dinna ken hoo ye make that oot, though; but gin there's tae be singin' ane must start, sae here goes: -

> "Ye've come too early to see us this year, John Frost,
> Wi' yer powther an' crispin' gear, John Frost,
> For hedge, tower, an' tree,
> As far's I can see,
> Are as white as the bloom o' a pear, John Frost."
> (-etc.)

"It's yer turn noo. Come gie's yer fav'rite."

"A'richt; ye ken what's comin': -

"It was one evening in the month of June,
The stars shone bright, the sky was clear;
The darkie played a good old tune
To serenade my Sally dear.

I lightly touch'd the banjo string,
Beneath the window that she might hear;
When soon the shutters back did swing,
And there I saw my Sally dear.

Then come, love, come, you need not fear,
My boat lies on the other shore;
And all I want is Sally dear,
And I'll be off to Baltimore."

Then, by agreement, we commenced together, -

"It fell aboot the Martinmas time,
An' a gay time it's then, O,
When oor guidwife had puddin's to mak',
An' she boiled them in the pan, O.
The wind blew cauld frae North tae South,
It blew into the floor, O;
Said oor guidman tae oor guidwife –
'Get up an' bar the door, O!
The barring o' oor door weel, weel, weel,
The barring o' oor door weel!'"

"I rapps you," exclaimed Birdie, (just as the indignant goodman was about to
confront the 'two gentlemen', and suffer the penalty of the "paction" to fall on
himself, by saying, -

"Wad ye kiss my wife afore my een,
An' scaud me wi' puddin' bree, O?")

pointing as he spoke to a long dark object lying on the sands a bittie seaward.

"An' what think ye it is?" I asked as we hastened to the spot – "what the deuce was
I lookin' at that I didna see it sooner!"

"By Jove!" said my cronie, "It seems a log of nae sma' size."

46

He was right; for when we reached it, it proved to be a sound log about fifteen feet long by a foot broad. We had scarcely surveyed the log, however, than our attention was drawn from it to innumerable other pieces of wood further on, which we soon discovered to be wedges of hard solid wood, varying from a foot to about three feet in length; and we were soon jumping about shouting – " I rapps this!" – and so on, until we got quite hoarse and dry throated, and didn't know very well which was the one's and which was the other's property.

"Did ever ye see the like o' this, Birdie," I at length took time to say; "why, man, we've cartloads o' the best firewood here at a whaup."

"Aye!" responded my enraptured cronie, "This is the luckiest tide I e'er kent – we maun hire a cairt the morn, I'm thinking."

"Atweel, there's mair nor ony cairt in Aberlady could haud, let alane what ony o' the auld nags could draw; - but what can we dae wi' oor wedges enoo?"

"Oh, I wad think they'll be safe eneuch lying there till the morn's morning, Jock; an', of course, we'll tak' hame what we can the nicht. But let's hae a look at the log again."

So we returned to the log, and after trying in vain to raise it from the ground, we secured it by driving some wedges into the sands at the sides of it, whereafter Birdie cut his initials on it with a clasp knife. We then sat down on it for a twinkling to congratulate one another on our extraordinary luck, and contemplate what was next to be done. At last we resolved to proceed a bit further along the shore, for, as Birdie remarked, there was no saying what we might yet find. When we had gone a short distance, I got a glimpse of something long lying a good bit ahead, scarcely yet visible, and shouted the invariable, "I rapps you, nae hauvers, nae squecks!"

"Anither log or I'm a Dutchman!" said my mate when he clapped his eyes on it.

It was found to be a plank that I could easily lift on my shoulders; so, after raising the toe end of it on a block of wood which lay at hand, so that we might easily see it on our return, we again proceeded. We had gone about half a mile without finding anything more of consequence, when an immense string of wild geese – very common there in winter – began to descend quite close to us. in a jiffy we had our slings, which we generally carried, out of our pouches and ready for use; but, alas, hardly a stone was to be had, even to replace them in our pooches; while the geese were making such a noise that we could hardly hear each other speak.

47

"I say, Birdie," said I, "there's plenty o' yer kith an' kin there, eh? – the gabblin' brutes!"

"Na, na!" returned Birdie, "they dinna belang tae oor clan o' Birds; but, dae you no' think they're in some respects like yersel'? Unco web-fitted, at ony rate."

"Web-fitted or no' web-fitted, lad, I'm no' a bird so I canna weel be a goose. But I'm thinking we may turn noo, a' the luck seems tae be nearer hame the nicht."

As my cronie acquiesced in the proposal, we retraced our steps homeward, I taking the plank found last, putting my bag round the middle of it and then shouldering it; while Jim filled his bag with as many wedges as he could carry. After many a long and toilsome stretch, and many a welcome and needful rest, we reached home with our burdens, with very sore backs and tired limbs, but light and proud hearts, and before bidding other "guid-nicht" resolved to set out with a hired cart early next morning.

I may state that when we arrived with a cart at the spot of our previous night's fortunes, we had the mortification to see that there was not a wedge left on the shore, all having been swept away by the morning tide, or lifted by some folk, who, though very unlikely, might have been there after we left the night before. Birdie's log, however, being still there, was hoisted into the cart and transported to the foot of the Wynd.

Chapter XVIII

One Friday night in the following December I waited at the foot of the Wynd for my inseparable cronie, Jim Bird, according to promise. I was well covered up, for the night was a snell one. I had a big coat close buttoned on me, and a scarf wrapped twice round my head. I hadn't waited a minute till I heard a whistle in the Wynd, to which I replied, and immediately heard a pair of feet come pattering down the road – and brawly I knew the owner.

"Guid e'en' tae ye Birdie!"

"Guid e'en! This is an awfu' nicht, Jock. Dae ye think we suld venture roon' the shore in sic a storm?"

"Hoot aye! Gin ye're game."

"I'm game."

So we set off, empty-handed, however –

"An sic a nicht tae tak' the road in,
As neir pair sinner was abroad in!"

The lift, or rather the clouds, were as black as pitch though, at sundry times, a slight break in them varied their aspect; and it was long yet till the hour of the moon rising. The bitter cutting wind was blowing strong and fiercely from the nor'-east, driving hilly showers of sleet before it; and eerily it souched through the bare trees of "McKay's Walk". The sea was a good bit up, though still coming in, and rougher than it had been for a long time, the waves lashing and splashing with ceaseless noise among the stones below the strip of grass. At first, we felt the wind extremely cold, which made us freeze and we almost resolved to turn; but as we went on at a sharp pace, we became a wee bit warmer.

When we reached the brig we had to use some caution, for in the extreme dark we could scarcely see the slaps in the sparring; and the sea being very high up, to fall in at that time perhaps would see us drowned. Leaving the brig behind and getting on to the sands, we felt the cold more than ever, for the nor'-east wind blows across the Bay at its utmost unchecked fury. Our hands, though in our pouches, were getting numbed by the cold, our eyes and noses were running, and our ears were nipping like mad. We passed several pieces of wood, only turning them over with our feet to see what like they were, and then go on. Scarcely ever did we speak to one another, except at intervals to say, "Oh my lugs!" – "This is awfu'!" or such like expressions but struggled on against the snell wind, while turning to take a breath, or to blow such as we had on our perishing hands; and, as for singing as was our normal routine, it never entered our heads, or if it did, we deemed it advisable to keep our mouths shut.

In this plight we reached a large crate, and turning it on end, and placing the open side towards the south, we began to make a temporary shelter by putting sheets of matting and bit of dales, which happened to be lying at hand, round it. We then made some attempts to kindle a fire of straw and chips of wood, but, after expending a lot of matches in vain, we gave it up as a bad job, the materials being over damp to take hold.

"Confound the things!" I exclaimed, scattering them with a fierce kick. "A'thing is gaun against us thegither the nicht; an' there's a shooer o' sleet comin' on – jist look at what black it is, blacker than ever, if possible."

"Ay, aye, Jock, there it comes – hooh, hooh! – I bet we're aye sheltered a wee bittie though no' muckle, God kens! That wind wad pierce onythin', an' perish an

Eskimo. Hear at thae deuks flying ower there on their whistlin' wings? I wonner gin they dinna feel cauld the nicht?"

"Would I were them, gin they dinna."

"The same here, cronie, but, tae gie ye a bit o' mind," he added, "I think we suld mak' the best o' oor way hame noo."

"Oh, bide a wee or that shooer's ower – see, it looks a kennin' lichter i' the north," I returned.

We did wait for a minute or two; but then the wind blew a very hurricane, making the matting spin away into the darkness, and, but for our combined weight, would have couped the crate easily. Having now little or no shelter, we lingered there no longer, but began a brisk pace towards home. We were hoping to take a piece of wood with us under our oxters, but after carrying it for a few yards we had to relinquish the effort, as our arms grew almost powerless.

When we placed the spot where we had sheltered as far behind us as the brig was still before us, Birdie drew close to my side, saying in a low voice – "Yonder's somethin' movin', as shure as guns! What on earth can it be?"

"Hoots!" I responded. "Ye're dreamin' man. – Na, fegs, I see it myself. I'll swear its somebody unco fain tae be there in sic a nicht."

"Umph!" said my mate, adding almost in a whisper, "Its no spring-heel'd Jack onyhoo. Whate'er it is, it disna seem tae be white. Oh, goodness! It's comin' this way. I've my big knife ready. Ha'e ye yours, Jock? We must stick thegither, whate'er it is."

"Man, ye make me fair feard, Birdie; it's aiblins naebody waur nor oorsel's. "

Keeping a close eye on the object of our dread, we turned our steps a good bit further west than we would otherwise have done, so as to elude, if possible, the strange apparition. It was in vain as the object seemed to hurry after us and, although we almost ran in our breathless terror, the distance between it and us became shorter and shorter. We were just about to make a wild race for home as a last resource, when to our unutterable joy, a voice came from the dreaded object with the words – "Is that you Jim?"

"Ay, aye!" exclaimed he of that name, in unlimited ecstasy, "It's my faither, thank Heaven!"

I here breathed a deep sigh of relief, for we had both got a sore fright, while the father, who quickly approached us, asked the son "What in a' the world are ye daein' here in siclike weather?"

"Oh, jist what we're aye daein'. But what brocht you here?"

"What's brocht me here? – What would it be but to seek for you, ye stravaigin' scoondrel! An' I was hauf expectin' tae be fa'in' ower yer corpse somewhere or ither, or tae be perished tae death mysel' i' the search. An' you tae (turning to me)? I wonner ye werena feard tae venture ower the doorstep in sic a foul nicht."

Feard?" answered my cronie, "There's no sic a word in his dictionary."

"A truce wi' yer nonsense," rejoined the father; "an' c'way hame as fast as ye like."

That we did, and soon reached the brig, over which we found the waves were constantly lashing, about a foot above the gangway. Here's another bonnie plight, we thought.

"We'll have tae gang 'yont tae the new brig," said the elder Bird.

"Oh, no," returned the other, "let's bide here a wee till the sea gangs back."

"We'd be perished waitin', man" said his father, "so we'd better shift at ance."

"I'm no' gaun roon' there," mumbled my cronie.

"Nor I," I put in.

"What else can we dae, ye gowks!" exclaimed the father, getting angry.

"Weel, I'll tell ye," said I; "hame's no' sae far awa' noo, an' we'd sune get oor buits an' stockin's off ance there, so let's gang ower even though we get wet feet."

"Ah, Johnny, lad" replied the elder Bird, "ye little ken the scaith resultin' frae wet feet; but I think we may tak' off oor buits an' wade it."

By this, however, I had started to cross; Jim followed; and after vain protestations so did his father. We got over a good deal drier than we expected, but still not

52

altogether dry-shod. Another five minutes hard walking brought us to the foot of the Wynd, where we had to part.

"Right gled am I we're this length," said I. "I'll see ye i' the mornin', Jim?"

"A'richt. Guid nicht!"

"Guid nicht!"

When I opened the room door, after passing the lobby, the light of the blazing fire and the gas almost blinded me, being so long in such darkness; but never was I gladder to find myself in a comfortable room. I found my mother and the rest of them in a wild state of anxiety on my account, but they soon forgot it in their joy at seeing me safe; and after getting my toes toasted, I went cantily to my bed, where, needless to say, I slept as sound as a top.

Chapter XIX

Next morning after porridge-time (for I didn't rise till then, being very weary after my previous night's exertions), I went over the gate to look if my cronie was to be seen anywhere. Looking up the Wynd I saw him standing at the head of it speaking to another school-mate, and very intimate cronie too, mentioned in a previous chapter – Jack Heriot. Giving a wag with my hand they both came down, while I went a wee bit to meet them.

"Well, Birdie," said I, "hoo do ye feel this mornin' efter last nicht's work?"

"Oh, fient a haet the waur, binna a kennin' tired. Are you gaun' ower enoo?"

"I think we may an' Heriot will come wi' us, eh?"

"Whaur?" asked Heriot, "Roon' the shore? I daursay I micht dae a hantle waur."

"A'richt," said Birdie and I in one breath.

"Will ye no' take a poke or somethin' though? added the former.

"Och!" I replied, "We'll trust tae get biggish pieces. We saw some last nicht that hae a chance to be there still."

"Well, let's aff," – and off we went.

A great improvement had taken place in the weather since the preceding night, and the morning was comparatively mild. The late storm, however had an impression on the surroundings – many big branches and one tree had been blown down; a lot of the deal planks piled in the joiner's yard, and the "auld wife" on one of the Wynd houses, had met the same fate, while the sea, now on the ebb, was very rough, and had a drumbie, sandy appearance. We had scarcely crossed the Brig when we observed a wounded duck make for the water; and of course, we immediately gave chase. Seeing that we intercepted its way to the sea the poor beast made a vain and pitiable waddle to beat us in the opposite direction. Heriot and I were hoping to catch it alive, but Birdie, outstripping us in the race, threw a piece of wood with all his pith at the unfortunate creature, and killed it on the spot.

"What a bonnie bird it is," he said, lifting and stroking its warm back. "Despite its broken wing, it's as good as eighteen pence ony day; an' I'll have ane o' these feathers stuck in my bonnet," plucking out the curled feathers at its tail – for it was a drake. Then after a pause, he addressed me – "I say, dae ye mind o' yon hare?"

"Ay, brawly that," I answered.

"What was't?" asked Heriot.

"Weel," said I, "I'll tell ye. A'e braw summer mornin' Birdie an' I forgaithered unco early at the fit o' the Wynd and turned oor staps tae the sea-side. When we reached the 'Bellfire Knowes' we spied a hare sportin' aboot jist ower the brae a bit and gey near the water's edge, the sea being gey high, whyles nibblin' awa' at the grass,

> "Or, thochtfu' like to mak' her brisker,
> Brushin' wi' dew her lang grey whisker,
> But pussie hadna sported lang,
> That morn the dewy grass amang,"

ere my cronie an' I secured a stoot cudgel each we stealthily made for the puir helpless creature. Ta'en by surprise at oor approach, the dumfoonert hare gien twa-three lowps, an' gaed helter-skelter intae the sea, to the edge o' whilk we ran, an' thus cut off its chance o' escape. After rushin' about back and forrit i' the water for a while – for I couldna ca' it swimmin' – hapless puss was drooned. My chum lost nae time in takin' aff his buits an' stockin's an' wadin' in for it. Sae, you see, we didna rise early for nocht that mornin'."

"Atweel no'," Heriot returned emphatically.

We now made for the shore, which wasn't long reached when Heriot lifted something in great haste and then made some fantastic gestures, from which Birdie and I concluded it must be something of rare worth in his opinion, at any rate.

"A purse! A purse!" he exclaimed in the greatest glee.

"Open it, then, an' let's see what's in't," suggested my cronie.

"I second that motion," said I, "the pruif o' the puddin''s the preein' o't."

So pressed, he opened it, and discovered all its contents to be a little cut Cavendish. The purse itself, however, was a good one and, as we proposed, we'd get a pipe and have a smoke of the "cut" bye and bye. Meanwhile, we resumed our search.

"I rapps you!" I exclaimed, observing a square looking object like a kist in the distance.

"An', I rapps this," said Birdie springing forward and lifting a fine piece of mahogany; then seeing me lift something asked "whit's that?"

"A gowff ba', a'maist split new," I replied letting him see it.

We found a considerable quantity of firewood, etc., before we reached the object I had claimed. That proved to be a common fish-box, strongly built, with a lid, and rope handles at each end.

"A rare box," said I, "but unco heavy."

"Well-I-wat – I rapps you!" exclaimed Birdie, pointing to something lying out on the wet sands."

"Gey like a lantern," thought Heriot.

"As like an auld tin can," I returned.

"I hope its something better, tho'" said Birdie, as he cantered off to see.

He soon reached it, and we saw him lift and examine it, then, hugging it in his arms, came running towards us, with the joyful exclamation – "a canister o' tea!"

"A canister it certainly is," I returned; "an' a guid sized ane tae boot; but for the tea; I think it's as likely to be fu' o' sand an' water."

"I wad say wi' you Jock," said Heriot.

We'll soon see aboot that," rejoined my other cronie, trying to get off the lid.

Meanwhile I had a good look of the tin canister, on the side of which was a Chineman sitting cross-legged who, Heriot declared, was very like Birdie's father; on the other side were letters and figures we couldn't make out at all; and on the other two sides were various Chinese designs, all being in gilt on a black background. After a long and hard struggle we got off the lid, which revealed to us two-three pounds of good tea; and wonderful to say, it was quite dry. I need not try to describe the joy of my cronie at his unprecedented find, but will proceed round the shore. Among other things we found were a straw mattress that had seemingly once served some poor sailor's bed, a fisherman's oilskin hat – called in some places a 'sou-waster', an oar, a sleeper, and a big sea-fowl called a scart or cormorant, all which, except the oar, we left lying, the bed and the "sou-waster" being useless, the sleeper over heavy, and the scart, stale. Somewhat further on Jack Heriot found a hand-barrow, apparently a mason's.

"This is aboot the place we got sic a fleg last nicht, Jock," said Birdie.

"What gien ye the fleg?" asked my other cronie, who'd to be told all about it.

"I think we suld turn hamewards noo," suggested the former, after telling Heriot the previous night's adventure.

"Oh aye," I returned, "ye're wearyin' tae free the contents o' the canister, nae doot?"

"An' what for no? But I'm shure we've a' got as muckle as we can take hame today at ony rate."

"Well, hame we'll gae then," Heriot and I at once acquiesced.

At Heriot's proposal we piled all the articles we intended to take on the hand-barrow, as we came to them. We took shifts at the carrying, as only two could conveniently carry the barrow; and in this manner we won home with a big load of as valuable stuff as we ever lifted from the sea-shore.

Chapter XX

One other Saturday morning, a good while after that related in the preceding chapter, I set out looking for the same old cronie. We had been round the shore the night before, and had agreed to meet early in the morning for our invariable round; but I, being far later than the appointed time, soon learnt that he had gone off himself with his sister about an hour earlier. I didn't waste a minute in hurrying after him, crossed the burn by the steps mentioned before, and over the sands as hard as I was able. When I had passed 'the hinmaist hole oot' on the golf green, I met him coming this way, whistling "Katy Beardy" as happy as a lark.

"Well," he accosted me, "what dae ye think o' my luck this mornin'?"

"What luck?" I asked.

"Did ye no meet my sister?"

"Na, I did not. I cam' ower the steps, an" I s'pose she'd go ower by the brig".

"Weel, dae ye see?" pointing to the shore near Jova's Neuk.

"I micht see't wi' half an e'e"

"An' what think ye it is then?" my cronie proceeded to question me.

"Troth!" I replied, "I dinna ken. But it looks unco like the ruit o' some muckle tree, or a piece of some wreck, or ane o' those diseased nowt that are bein' washed in here enoo."

"Na, na!" he returned, "it's naethin' mair nor less nor a boat – a Norwegian skiff."

"A boat!" I exclaimed. "Is that a fac'?"

"As fac' as death! And mair nor that, there's nae muckle wrang wi't. It's lyin' keel upmaist, - we'll no can turn it till my faither comes; I sent my sister hame for him, and he'll no' be lang, I'se warrant ye."

We now cantered off to the boat, which we soon reached, and I had a good look of it, when I saw that my chum hadn't deceived me in saying there was little wrong with it. As for Birdie, he could speak of nothing else.

"Isn't this a glorious find," said he, "we'll no' need poke nor rope for oor sticks noo, Jock, for we'll can ferry them a' ower in this skiff - that'll be gran'."

"Dinna craw so croose, my man," I retorted, "it's owner aiblins no' agree with your suggestion; and, at ony rate, the coast-guard will hae tae be consulted."

"A ban on the coast-guard! And as for its owner, I'm no. fear'd for 'im turnin' up; - but, see! Yonder comes my faither."

When the latter had arrived and got a good look of Jim's lucky find, the three of us managed to turn it on its keel, and only awaited the tide, and wanted oars to take it a wee nearer home. We had a long time to wait yet before the sea would come near the boat, which interval was occupied in seeking for some oars. Proper oars we couldn't get, but got two pailing rails, which, after rounding the ends a bittie, we deemed would stand in their stead; and we also made two pairs of rowing pins that were needed too. At length and long, the sea came within a few yards of the skiff, and impatient of waiting, we put our combined strength into shoving her into the water.

"Shove-a-hoy! – shove-a-hoy! There we are noo, afloat on the heavin' wave – jump in, my lads!"

The boat was no sooner afloat than my cronie and his father got seated to the oars.

"It's lucky," said the elder, "that we brought that pannikin, as I see the auld thing's leakin'."

"I'll bail oot the water," said I, which I did, and was kept almost constantly at it. We had to go somewhat to the west before we could direct the bow towards Aberlady and steer right across. in a while I noticed my cronie was getting very tired keeping stroke with his father, so I proposed, being bigger and stronger than he, that we should change places. As he readily agreed I took his resigned oar, and after long and protracted rowing we landed the skiff safely on the turf, opposite the foot of the Wynd, in the presence of a large concourse of laddies and lassies, who had come to see "the boat that Birdie faund." It's owner never turned up, and so, after paying the coast-guard at North Berwick, it became the sole property of the Birds.

For many a day Birdie's boat was moored near the place we had first stranded it – at the 'pipes'. We often got a sail in it about the bay, and sometimes brought a load of sticks in it, as my cronie had suggested. Nevertheless, I once got a bit sail in it I'd scarcely reckoned upon, and it happened in the following manner. One morning, about and hour before school-time, I took a wander down to the sea-green. The sea was very well in, and Birdie's boat was floating very tempting like, so for it I turned my steps. I made my way along a miniature breakwater, close to which the skiff was tied to a short stab fixed in the sand for the purpose, and reaching over as far as I could, got hold of the rope and pulled the boat to where I was standing. I jumped in, and, as the rope by which she was moored was somewhat lengthy, diverted myself with alternatively shoving her out and pulling her in again – for you know, 'little pleases bairns'. Happily, I gave her a shove with all my pith, and for a jiffy stood really pleased with the rate I had propelled her through the water; but it soon struck me she was going very far. Instinctively, I seized on the rope and gave it such a pull that I landed on my back in the bottom of the boat among a lot of dirty water! In a minute, however, I was to my feet, and immediately recognised my predicament - the rope had come loose. By this time the boat was in very deep water and some distance from the shore, and still going the further out, as it was a back going tide; so, with hardly an oar or even a spar, you may guess I didn't feel altogether easy. As nobody was near to see or help me, I was left to my own endeavours; and hitting a plan, I took off the boot and stocking of my right foot, tucked up that leg of my knickerbockers as far as they'd go, and facing the west, the direction the boat was going, thrust that leg into the water and paddled with it like fury. Oh, happy was I to see that this had the desired effect in propelling the boat into the shallow water, where it was an easy matter to run her aground. Securing her as well as I could, I again put on my boot and stocking, with a sigh of relief at being once more on *terra firma*, then hastened home for my books, and thence to the school, for which I was rather late, but never let on what had kept me to anybody.

Chapter XXI

Our quite little clachan, with its irregularly built street, and all its outhouses, vennels, garden plots, trees, shrubs, etc., was just about as favourable a place as could be for our favourite winter night's game. "The Hounds an' the Tod."

This game we used to call – and the laddies in Aberlady still call it – 'The Fox an' the Tod', but that name is quite incongruous, fox and tod being the same thing, and so I think the name I've given above must be what is meant, and a glisk of the game might almost confirm it. Say, then, that the seven of us laddies met, as the gloaming gave place to night, for a game at 'Hounds an' the Tod', two of us were let off as tods, (the number of pursuers always being on an average of three to one of the pursued), and the remainder were left as the hounds. The tods then set about hiding themselves, perhaps in some dark corner or vennel, or on the top of some coach-house or cellar, or among a pile of wood, or behind some dyke, or up some tree, or among some bushy shrubs, - for we didn't scruple to trespass in the folk's gardens, - and when snugly hidden they gave the shout "Tally-ho!" and then the hunt commenced. Sometimes it was took a long while before the tods were found, and sometimes as long before they were caught, when the operation of cutting off their tails was gone through; whoever accomplished this latter first was made a tod in the next hunt. Nothing in all the range of amusements I liked as well, at that time, as the above game, and many a time I played it in the greatest of glee with my dear old cronies.

Well, then, one Saturday night a many of us were playing at 'Hounds an' the Tod' in the hinter end of gloaming, when, after the first hunt, Birdie, who was among us, reminded me that it was Hallowe'en.

> "Some meery, freenly, countra folks,
> Thegither did convene,
> Tae burn their nits, an' pu' their stocks,
> An' haud their Halloween,
> Fu' blythe that nicht."

The night before, the scholars held their Hallowe'en in the school, had a lantern procession, and then a treat, but Birdie and I had resolved to hold a Hallowe'en by ourselves on the proper night, that was the Saturday. So when my cronie reminded me what night it was, I replied, "Aye, Birdie, ye're richt! I was amaist forgettin' aboot Hallowe'en, I'm aye sae ta'en up wi' that game; but noo sin' ye've pat it in my mind , let's awa' doon – I've got a big tub o' water an' apples a' ready for the dookin', and we'll burn oor nits, and pu' oor stocks" or 'kail-runts' as we call them "aifterwards, if we see fit."

With that I led the way down the Wynd and into our washing-house, where we got a candle lit, and then spent about an hour dooking for apples and other Hallowe'en pranks, then we returned up the clachan again, and met some chums who were standing at the lamp near the Cross discussing the day, and suggesting that we have a rise out of Andrew Dunlop, who kept a wee shop near the middle of the clachan, and had a temper about as short as himself, although he was a cantie, jokey body when not roused. Among the lower animals it is a common thing that the weak and infirm are treated with the most harshness by the others; and, though fortunately it is generally the reverse with human beings, still in this case, old Andrew, who had a good deal of infirmities to complain of, and did complain of, was most unmercifully tormented by us thoughtless youngsters. After some discussion we resolved to play on him the following Hallowe'en pliskie.

Having procured a pirn of thread, a pin, and a button, we stealthily approached the body's window, stuck the pin into the top of the lower sash, secured the end of the thread to it, fixed the button on the thread, so as it would hang down to the middle of the pane, and while one of us went to make sure all was right, and keep the button from rattling on the glass before the time, the rest of us slipped across the street, taking the pirn with us, and letting out the thread till it reached right across.

He that had waited at the window now joined us, and we all hid ourselves behind the little dyke and pailing opposite the shop.

Everything now ready, he who had a grip of the thread gave it two or three tugs, and we heard the button rattle against the glass pane. Andrew came bang out of his shop, making the bell at the door ring like fury, and rushed here and there to try and catch the offender; but, as nobody was to be seen, he returned into the shop, mumbling something we couldn't make out. He had scarcely time to be well in, when the rattling was repeated, and out he came again, cursing "thae d-----d nine year aulds", and threatening us with the jail; but though he searched each neuk this time, he couldn't find any culprits, so he returned again to the door, where he stood for some time before disappearing into the shop. Once more the button was made to rattle on the window; but Andrew didn't seem to heed it this time, so it was repeated, and out he came again, and went straight to the window. At length he noticed the button, and was about to grip it, when, through a timely tug of the thread, it vanished from his sight, leaving him in blank astonishment, and perhaps, 'tae gie the wyte o' the deed to the witches', which are said to be so rife on Hallowe'en.

When he had once more placed the shop door between himself and us, we sallied out of our hiding place, and proposed to play another pliskie on some of the other villagers, and that was, I may say at once, to whiten their windows. One of my cronies volunteered to get the whitening and I to get the dish to mix it in, and the piece of cloth with which to paint the windows. These gotten, and the whitening mixed up, we proceeded to make some very conspicuous figures on the folk's windows, chiefly the shop ones. With one exception, when we had to show some clean pairs of heels, we had, as yet, got safe off, though later I heard a certain shop-keeper, near the middle of the village, say to a customer when she observed her window had got the usual Hallowe'en decorations – "Weel, aweel, see my window; that cows the gowan; what a mess! I'se warrant ye, noo, it was that Johnny Reid, he's the wildest loon i' the place."

We now contemplated giving a dose to the shop in which we were before we flitted to the present house. It was tenanted at this time by Mr Henry Welch, a very irritable young man, on the score of being tormented by the laddies, at any rate. We had just completed the painting business, when, swith, out came Henry with a jug of water to throw about us. Of course, we were off like a shot, whenever we heard the door open; and our pursuer, aiming to give us some water about our lugs, in his eagerness the jug went slap out of his hands along with the water, and falling in the gutter, was smashed to a thousand pieces. As you may guess, that didn't sweeten his temper, and, with burning rage, and inaudible imprecation, he retreated to his shop-door. After a hearty laugh to ourselves, we were very imprudently approached quite near the shop of the injured and fiery Henry Welch. With his utmost speed, Henry made a dart upon us, to 'glut his ire' if possible by making an example of some of us; but, being on the alert, we were off at once like so many deer. Seeing we were very closely pursued, I threw the dish of whitening (which I had the misfortune to have at the time) across the road, so that I might run the easier. When we passed the Cross I gave a bit glimpse over my shoulder to see how the chase was likely to end, and observed that Henry still kept close on us, but had, however, passed some of my cronies in the wake, so thinking he would pass me too, I slackened my pace. But lack-a-day! I was far mistaken; for –

> "Like mountain cat that guards her young,
> Full at my luckless throat he sprung,"

He took such a tenacious grip of my coat, that I deemed it would be in vain to struggle with him; so I submitted to his mandate – "Come on, here!," as he half lead, half shoved, me in the direction of his shop. Well, well thought I! This is my bad luck again; if I hadn't had the dish of whitening it might have been different with me now, for I didn't put so much on his windows as my chums. But what worth such reflections? Leading me through the pend, and round the back of his house, he opened a cellar door, thrust me in with the brief exclamation, "There!" He locked the door, and left me to my own rueful meditations. Many, many a time had I been in that place before, but under very different circumstances, and it being 'pick mirck', I went tumbling forward among coal, sticks, paraffin oil barrels, etc., in no enviable state of mind, you may be sure. Finding my way again to the door I began to kick at it with the utmost fury. After having exerted myself for some time in this way to no purpose, I desisted; the story coming into my mind about the prisoner who got his boots taken off for the same thing, and then told to kick away as much as he liked. As my anger vanished, fear approached, and I was just about giving way to the latter, when the lock was turned, the door opened, and I stepped out to confront my late captor.

"Ye may gang awa' hame, noo," said he, "an' thank yer stars the bobbie's no' at hame the nicht!"

> "I only said, 'imph-m',
> That awfu' word 'imph-m',
> That auld Scots word 'imph-m',
> Ye ken it means aye"

and hooked it away home as quick as I could. Oh, well do I mind, and shall always mind while blessed with memory, that Hallowe'en when I was locked in Welch's cellar. Served me right, do you say?

Chapter XXII

In the vicinity of Aberlady is one of the foremost golf greens in Scotland, on Luffness Links – it being generally considered second to, if not equal to, that at St Andrews. This fact brings many enthusiastic players of 'the royal and ancient game' from Edinburgh in particular, but many other towns considerably further, to boot, in order to get a day's enjoyment at their favourite pastime.

I have stated heretofore that we laddies were overjoyed at any feasible excuse to win away from the school; and a very common and aft longed for excuse was, that we were wanted to act as caddies to those gentlemen. One day, then, some five or six of us had been carrying clubs, and in that way earned about eighteen pence the piece, with which we suggested, and thereafter resolved, to have a bit spree among ourselves.

The place selected for our jollification was the nor'-west side of the 'Bellfire Knowes'; and we soon got a lot of biscuits, with herring, cheese, and small beer. We then gathered a quantity of sticks, etc., and made a fire, on which we proceeded to roast the red herring. While these were in process of cooking, one of my cronies, Tam G---, proposed that we should have some tatties to eat along with them; and he and another set off to a neighbouring field to fetch some, while I volunteered to get a pot. I wasn't long in returning with that utensil, having got hold of an old one without the lid; though my cronies were there before me with the tatties. These we put in the pot, having previously three-quarters filled it with sea-water – which required no salt – and placed it on the blazing fire. Nevertheless, our fuel was exhausted before the tatties were yet half ready, and a discussion followed, the result of which being the resolution to supply our want, by partially breaking up an old bread van belonging to Willie Wilson of the Wynd, and standing along the green about thirty yards from us. That we did with anything we could lay hands on, bars of iron and big stones being our chief implements, and kept the fire crackling around the pot till its contents were ready.

The tatties were wild, braw and mealy and we soon made a lot of them disappear along with the herring; but, our appetites getting satiated and a quantity of the tatties being still left, we began to argue about the remainder. When the last of the spuds had been thus wasted, we returned to our fire, and did full justice to the biscuits and cheese, not forgetting the beer. Nor did we leave off our feasting and doffing till darkness had spread over the face of nature, when we returned to the village to have a game at 'Hounds an' the Tod', before we ultimately went home to glimpse at our lessons for the next day. Aft, aft, and for long after, when we met at some street-lamp or window of some shop at night to have a crack, our herring spree was always a welcome though much hackneyed theme, and we reviewed it with a cherished fondness we couldn't suppress; but Willie Wilson never found out, to my knowledge, who it was that broke his old van.

The first day of April, All Fool's Day, or 'Hunt-the-Gowk', as it is better known with us, was always a day on which we had to keep alert, lest we should bring upon us the rhyme –

"Hunt the Gowk, April,
Send the gowk anither mile",

for among us youngsters it was a day of wanton imposition and deception throughout. It was then a common sight to see a man or woman or youngster go stalking about, quite unconscious of the paper appendage pinned behind them; and oh, it was glorious fun if we managed to pin a bit to the master's coat-tail - behind his back, of course! 'Hunt-the-Gowk' about this time fell on a Saturday, when my mother and grandmother were away at Slateford, and I was left under the charge of my cousin. Now, Birdie and I were aiming to play about the house; but, before we could manage that we thought it advisable to get the place to ourselves, if possible, so I declared I would get rid of, for a while, my temporary guardian. Entering the house with as long a face as possible, I told her that Miss Craven (a dressmaker in the village with whom she was very chief) wanted to see her, if she'd come up as soon as she could. That seeming quite natural, my cousin gave herself a bit snod up and very 'heich', went on her way to her friend's. As soon as she disappeared round the corner of the Wynd, I rejoined my cronie, laughing in my sleeve at the 'Hunt-the-Gowk' I had given Miss Maggie.

Our little pliskie over, we left the house and went round the sea-green; but when I returned Maggie was standing at the gate , and before I had time to ask her if she had seen Miss Craven, told me that my Aunty had some rubbish she was wanting me to take down to the sea in the barrow. Without thinking anything about it, I hastened for the barrow, and ran it up to the Cross Cottage. There, of course, I asked my Aunty where the rubbish was, that I was to hurl to the sea; but she said she didn't think she had much but would look. At that I wondered, you may guess, but never for a minute suspected the truth. She did look for rubbish, but returned, saying that if I came back some other day she might have a barrowful for me, but she couldn't very well give it to me just now.

"Very weel", I returned, and went away down to the house again, where Maggie was still standing at the gate.

"Weel, whaur's the rubbish?" she accosted me, with a big smile on her face; and, for the first time, a new light dawned in my 'harran-pan', and I had a hearty laugh at my own stupidity.

Chapter XXIII

Almost each night in the month of June previous to the 'Race', might be seen a gathering of young laddies practicing for the Games, on the village green or common. We younger laddies sometimes looked on, and envied much of the agility displayed by some of our seniors; but just as often, I dare say, we tried our own powers among ourselves at running, jumping in its various forms, and vaulting. It was when trying my hand at the last-named that I got a mishap one night, that rendered me unable to walk, or attend school, for some two or three weeks. The cross-bar was up about six feet, and one of my rivals had just gone over it without knocking it down, so I determined to exert my full powers to do likewise. With that purpose I seized the pole, and after taking a survey of the turf from which I was to spring, I made a short race, and strained every muscle as I gave the vault. I barely cleared it, though the cross-bar remained in its place; but, wow me! In throwing myself over, I had turned my body three quarters round about, and now came thud down on a stone or something with one of my feet. In a moment I was lying on the green, enduring the severest pain in my ankle; and I could hardly suppress the inclination to roar and greet. Finding the pain was not merely momentary, and had no appearance of mitigation, I, with great difficulty, got to my feet, and hobbled away home like a hen with a coweredly leg. My chums, who hadn't noticed the accident, roared after me, "What's wrang wi' ye, Reidie?" to which I could only force myself to answer, "I've hurt ma fit." When I got into the house, I threw myself down into a chair, and proceeded to take off my boot, and by the time I got it off, my mother was on the scene.

Though at first I tried to hide from her what had happened, it was of no use; and so, judging from the gestures and grimaces I was making that it was something serious, she immediately sent for my grandfather. The doctor arrived, and after examining my ankle, pronounced it to be a very bad sprain, and gave directions as to what was to be done with it. That night there was little or no sleep for me, as I lay and moaned and groaned most of the time. Next morning the pain wasn't much better, and my ankle swelled like 'a horse's leg with a weed', in addition to being blue and purple. All that day I was confined to bed, but next afternoon I was helped to a reclining position on the sofa. There I had a fine view of the green, and before long a number of my chums arrived there to try their skill at some of the athletic sports.

After having a race and a 'hap-stap-an-loup' competition, they put up the posts to have a trial at vaulting. They had continued that for some time, and the cross-bar had been raised to about the same height as that which cost me dear only two nights previous, when I observed my friend Birdie take the pole for his turn. "Noo, then, my lad", thought I, "tak' tent ye dinna get yer ankle sprained like me." The thought had scarcely escaped my mind, when Birdie's hand s slipped on the pole, and down he fell. Immediately there was a gathering round him followed by his being led from the green in an apparent disabled condition. Of course, I was anxious to know what had happened, but couldn't move myself. However, I soon heard to my disconsolation that my cronie had dislocated his arm. Two-three days after this, I was able to go a wee bittie, with the assistance of a long-handled broom, which I used as a crutch, but couldn't yet put my foot on the ground. I had got the length of the outside gate, and rested for a minute on the dyke and pailing when, presently, Birdie came down the Wynd with his arm in a sling; and a neither of us could keep from laughing at the circumstances under which we met that day.

"Nae mair vaultin' for us for a whyle, my lad," was my greeting.

"Na, forsooth; but nae mair schule either, man. What think ye o' that?"

"Oh, its weel eneuch for ye that can gang aboot, but gey wearisome for me that canna. But, c' awa' up tae the gairden and we'll hae a crack."

So we adjourned to the garden, where we, not without some difficulty, erected a seat for ourselves, on which we soon were seated, with a stalk of rhubarb each; and discussed our respective accidents, and the suffering we had to endure.

"Weel, aweel", said I, after some time, "seeing we canna sing here a' thegither, come, gie's a guess or a story."

"A guess?" responded my chum; "Here ye are, then - why does a coo look ower a dyke?"

"Oh, we a' ken that; gie's some new ane, or else tell a story."

"I dinna mind o' ony jist noo, Jock. Hae ye nane yerself?"

"Weel, aweel, then," said I; "here's a gey guid anecdote gin I dinna spoil it in the tellin'. A laddie, who'd been amusin' himself' on the quay at a certain seaport harbour, accidentally fell intae the water, whilk at the time was unco deep. A bystander, havin' seen him, rushed tae the spot, an' was fortunate in rescuing the laddie before he had suffered muckle mair nor a guid dookin'. On comin' tae himsel', the laddie turned to his deliverer wi' an expression o' the sincerest gratitude, an' said, "Oh, man, I'm awfu' gled ye gat me oot. What a lickin' I wad hae gat frae my mither gin I had been drooned!"

"Ha, ha, ha! Ca' cannie, man. Ye've garr'd me hurt my airm wi' lauchin'", exclaimed my mate. "Noo, I suppose its my turn, sae here's mine. A stoot, respectably dressed woman entered an omnibus in Edinburgh a'e day short syne;

but a' the seats were completely filled. Lookin' roon' aboot her, ane o' the passengers remarked, 'Hae ye naethin' tae sit doon on, honest woman?' 'I hiv something tae sit doon on', was her indignant reply, 'but I dinna see where tae put it.'"

"Oh, that'll dae Birdie", said I. "But here's anither.' Gie's twa eggs for my denner", demanded a woman o' a grocer a'e day. Noo, it had been an a'maist daily thing wi' her tae get the twa eggs for the same purpose, so the counter-louper spiered at her, in a cannie way 'Ye're surely a vegetarian, Mrs ------?' 'Na, na' she replied, 'I'm nae vegetarian; I'm a staunch U.P!' Come on, man! Keep the puddin' warm!"

"Aye, aye, here's ane mair. An auld shepherd chiel, once paid a visit tae an acquaintance, and took wi' him his little grandson; an' for the latter this was the first time he had been any length frae his mountain hame. While his grandsire was haein' a crack on ither days wi' his auld freen' in the hoose, the younker daundered oot tae the gairden at the back tae enjoy himsel' there. Noo, there was a branch o' the local railway running close by the kail-yard, an' it happened that a passenger train passed while the laddie was lookin' aboot him. This he beheld wi' the greatest consternation, an' hastened into the hoose, roarin', 'Oh gran'faither, come here! There's a smiddie ran awa' with a row o' hooses!'"

"No bad; an', noo, here's an advertisement that appeared in the columns o' an Edinburgh newspaper: 'For Sale. A handsome piano, the property of a lady, who is leaving Scotland in a walnut case with turned legs'."

In such a way we passed away part of that afternoon; but, as our wounds began to ache, and it was close on tea-time, we had to separate but like Burns' dogs, 'resolved tae meet some ither day', an' that before long.

As time drove on, my ancient, trusty cronie and myself, were greatly recovered from our accidents; and in the case of my ankle, at least, it strengthened wonderfully.

Chapter XXIV

A good while before the accident related in the foregoing chapter, I had often acquainted with Peter McLaren, a hairum-skairum chiel' like myself, and awfully fond of explorations and adventures. Though somewhat smaller than I, for I was a big fellow for my years, he was a year and a half my senior. He lived at Ballencrieff with his brother, who had a market garden there, and therefore had to travel that distance, above two miles, back and forward to the school each day. Peter and I were now in the same class, and very often seated together, so we got very familiar, and rose by rapid strides in each other's favour and esteem. Our intimacy, which, had grown to the most confidential friendship, was still more enhanced by the marriage of my cousin, Miss Horsburgh, to the aforesaid brother of my new cronie. After this, until the time Peter left the district, he and I were scarcely ever separate in our hours of leisure; and many's the prank we played in the playground, the village, or the surrounding district!

The marriage above referred to hadn't long passed away, when my worthy grandfather was called to the great majority. He slipped from this world in the summer of 1874, 'deeply regretted by many attached friends', as the phrase goes. He was 77 years of age at his demise; yet, having being born on the 29th of February, 1796, he had only seen 19 birthday anniversaries – which number, exactly, and I have now seen myself. Few, if any individual, has been so sorely missed in and about Aberlady, as my grandfather, the doctor. It would be quite superfluous to say how well he was known, and how widely and highly he was respected. It had been his practice for many a year to make the sick and infirm throughout the place his daily care; he visited them all whether asked or not – whether in prospect of remuneration or not – and everywhere he was made welcome. But now the good old man lies with my father and many other friends in the deserted looking Kirk-yard of Gullane.

Among our extra school lessons at this time, we got a little botany, in the summer months at least; and this, I may say, was almost the only thing I ever liked at the school. It was the master's practice to bring in some weeds or garden flowers, so that he might ascertain what progress we were making in our study, by taking the plant to pieces and asking us to name the different parts, or tell to what class the root, the leaf, or the flower belonged, etc. One day – we must have been very far forward with our lessons at the time, I presume – our teacher sent four of us young botanists to Gullane Links, to search for, and bring to the school, a specimen of all the less common species of wild flowers that grew there, in order that they might undergo his and our inspection for beneficial purposes. He assigned us this pleasant errand as we came out the school at twelve o'clock; so the four of us, my chum, Peter McLaren, Will N----------, Wattie K---------, and myself, after leaving school, hastened home for our dinners, and then set off for the links in great glee.

After crossing the brig, we daundered on in the direction of Gullane, picking up some bits of flowering weeds on our way; and, as we had now approached very near that clachan, we agreed to pay it a brief visit. Having had a peep in at a little confectionery shop window, we turned up a lane that leads to the sea-side. Just a wee bit before we came in view of the Firth, I stopped my cronies to have a glimpse of an auld two-storeyed house to our right hand side, within a little gate, and in a kind of howe. It was the home of my ancestors. Its walls, like these of other old buildings, were of immense thickness, in comparison to the cockle-shells they build now-a-days, and almost entirely covered with ivy, its wee windows looking still less through the encroachments of 'that fine old plant, the ivy green'. It was occupied at the time by two aunts, sisters of my grandfather – rather eccentric bodies, but strictly devout.

Round about the house grew numerous herbs, cultivated by one of the inmates; and bunches of these plants might be seen hanging above the door to dry, for my auntie made out of them a kind of saw or ointment for the cure of sores, etc., which was reputed to be of no small value. At one time this locality was the scene of frequent sand-drifts, the sand being blown into large wreaths like that of snow; and in one of those sand-drifts the old house was so completely enveloped once, that the only exit left clear for the inhabitants was the sky-light window. That house was the home of my sires, as far back as I can trace. It became theirs about the time of the Reformation, previous to that which it had been the Roman Catholic manse. Since then it has ever been occupied by Reids, till three years ago, when the last of its occupants, in the person of one of the aforementioned aunts, was transported thence to her narrow bed in God's Acre. But this, I fear, is a digression.

Having had a short tour round Gullane, my three chums and I made our way past the Wheem, a small farmhouse on the top of the eminence dignified by the name of Gullane Hill, and away down to the western side of the links. After daundering about for some time, we found ourselves in close proximity to the sea-shore, about half way between the Golf House and Jova's Neuk, or, perhaps, a little nearer the latter. As the day was bright and warm, McLaren and I, being extremely fond of the water, resolved to have a dook. Our other two cronies wouldn't join in, but promised to wait till we got our dip. The sea was very far back, so Peter and I, after divesting ourselves of clothes, had a long way to run before we got to the water. Our bathing over, the four of us took another wander across the links a bit, and then headed for home, with two or three quite common wild flowers each. It was four o'clock when we reached the school, and our class was just on the eve of being dispersed for the day. We gave our plants to the dominie, who asked why we had been so long, and seemed very dissatisfied with what we had brought him; the result of it being that he never sent us on a like errand again.

Chapter XXV

It was a snell winter day, the scholars had been dispersed for dinner, when Peter McLaren and I, along with two or three other schoolmates, after hurrying past with our dinner, took the gate for the loch near the Golf House, at a canny canter. As the frost had been very keen for several days, the loch was quite bearable, and we laddies were soon flying about on the glass ice, not on fancy skates, but on good substantial tackety boots.

When folk are kept in a state of happy excitement, how swiftly the time seems to pass! Between various tricks, dodges, and cantrips, which I need not dwell on at length, we had a happy time of it.

> "As bees flee home wi' lades of treasure,
> The meenits wing'd their way wi' pleasure"

An'; though the day was snell and cold, before long we were sweating, and our faces and hands glowing like a Christmas fire.

> "But pleasures are like poppies spread,
> You seize the flow'r, its bloom is shed,
> Or, like the snow-fall in a river,
> A moment white, then melts for ever;
> Or, like the Borealis race,
> That flit ere you can point their place,
> Or, like the rainbow's lovely form,
> Evanishing amid the storm!"

Even so, in the meridian of our enjoyment, we were arrested by the far, faint sound of the familiar, but unpopular, school-bell. Each one, except McLaren and myself, took to their heels as soon as the first toll fell on their ears; but we two still remained, saying to our mates as they hurried off, that we would meet up on them before they reached the village, which, however, we did not, as will be seen from the sequel.

"Jist a'e mair turn roon' the loch," said Peter, and we scudded along the ice, like two pieces, or rather, drops, of mercury along the smooth surface of a table.

"D'ye see whaur they are?" I asked, when we were leaving the loch to take our homeward race. "We micht as weel try tae flee i' the air, as tae meet up wi' yon fellas noo; - see they're jist yairds frae the Wynd!"

"Odds, nouns! Ye're richt," returned my cronie. "An' I guess we may as weel gang back to oor slidin' again, an' tak' the remainder o' the day tae oorsel's, - the consequences will be muckle the same – a lickin' or a 'keep in' is amaist inevitable."

So we returned to our sport, and slid about on the ice, sometimes forwards, sometimes backwards, sometimes on one foot, sometimes hunkery-ways, for a while, to our hearts' content. Happily, we indulged in a game at football on the ice, which was a very fascinating, though rather dangerous, performance, and a bit of a novelty. Indeed, the game of football itself was almost new to us then, as it had

71

only been introduced amongst us scholars a few weeks previous, when we had formed a juvenile club, of which McLaren and I were captain and vice-captain, respectively. It was getting very grey when my cronie and I left the loch at a brisk walking pace for home; and, as he wouldn't go into our house on the way by, I accompanied him, as was my practice, up the road, the length of the 'Clattering Cassie', a brig over a wee burnie on the Aberlady side of the Brickworks. What is only called the Brickworks now, being a solitary building a little off the main road, as the brick and tile work was no longer carried out.

Next morning, when we had all marched into the school from the playground, where we assembled and had got seated on our respective forms, the dominie turned to us and said, "McLaren and Reid, come here: I wish to speak to you two." And when we had gone out to the middle of the floor, and there stood like two condemned criminals, he proceeded –

"How did it come that neither of you were present here yesterday afternoon?"

"Please, sir" said I, with a tremulous voice, "we were over at the loch at dinner time having a slide, and on our return to the school we crossed the burn, which was frozen over, but both of us fell through the ice, and got ourselves very wet. And, please sir, by the time we got our clothes dried, it was nearly time for the school being dispersed."

This statement was seconded by my cronie, Peter.

"Oh, God forgie us for leein', for leein',
Oh, God forgie us for leein'!"

Although none of our mates could corroborate the statement, at the same time none of them could contradict it, so the master, who had some suspicion regarding the truth of it, ordered us to stay in the school at night and after the others, which we did, and got our next day's lessons learned.

Chapter XXVI

"Couldna ye hae come a bittock farther, ye lazy lubber ye?" Such was the compliment with which my inseparable cronie, Peter McLaren, accosted me, one bonnie summer Saturday morning. The previous night, the two of us had agreed to meet at the 'Clattering Cassie" previously referred to, at ten o'clock next morning. As I had arrived there somewhat before the appointed time, I thought it needless to go farther, to meet my chum; and so, I sat me down on the parapet of the brig to await him. There I sat drinking in the exquisite music of the larks combined with

72

that of the tumbling burn below me, and had just began to crow over that beautiful Irish song, commencing – "I'm sitting on the stile, Mary," when my reverie was broken in the manner above described.

"Weel, McLaren," I replied to his off-hand greeting, "I micht hae come farther, sure eneuch; but, as I haena done sae, I dinna think there's muckle lost by't. What's gaun on up-bye? Tak' a seat for a meenit."

"Oh," was my cronie's response, "there is ne'er muckle gaun on up yonder. The coo calved last night, an' I believe it's a cuddy! But what's the guid o' sittin' here, Reidie? Let's tak' the gate. This is a rare day for oor trip, eh?"

"Couldna be better," I rejoined; "an' the sea'll be fu' atween ane an' twa o'clock, sae we'll catch it comin' in."

"Och, it doesna matter for that part whether the sea's comin' in or no' at Jovah's Neuk, there's aye rowth o' water there for dookin'; but, I daursay, its safest when the tide is on the flow."

We were just about to illustrate the truth of my cronie's last remark, as will be seen presently. The trip we contemplated taking, and, indeed, I may say, had started on, was to Jovah's Neuk, where we proposed spending a few hours; and we had provided ourselves with sandwiches for the occasion, which were safely stowed in our coat pouches. We soon reached Aberlady, *en route*, where I made the suggestion that, as the day was oppressively warm, we should relieve our feet of boots and stockings, and go bare-foot. This we did, leaving our boots in the house, *en passant*. We waded through the burn at the 'steps', and immediately were skelping over the wet, ribbed sands, in bright anticipation of a jolly day's doffing. Before long we began to feel the heat of the sun on our backs, as if there were a glowing furnace behind us, which made a free sweat break over our bodies, and made us peck like dogs.

"Its uncommonly close an' warm the day, McLaren," I remarked; "or, as 'Cabbie' wad pit it, unco close an' sharp. But yonder are some heavy lookin' clouds, I hope its nae gaun tae rain on us."

"I hope no," replied my cronie; "but its raither threatenin' like. –

> 'Oh, what a sultry sky is this I'm under,
> Yon ill-forboding cloud seems big with
> thunder!'"

"Halloah! Pate. Wha's that ye're quotin'? I'm shure that's no in any o' oor schule books."

"Ye think I ne'er read ony but schulel books? Weel apparently, ye dae; but, I ken I dinna. Nor wad I read them either, gin I could help it. Can ye say ony o' Monday's lessons?"

"Aye! I can say my Caesar – I'm Mark Antony, ye ken –

> 'Friends, Romans, countrymen, lend me your ears,
> I come to bury Caesar, not to praise him.
> The evil that men do lives after them;
> The good is oft interred with their bones;
> So, let it be with Caesar. The noble Brutus
> Hath told us Caesar was ambitious:
> If it were so, it was a grievous fault,
> And grievously hath Caesar answered it!'

An' troth, I think I can repeat my French grammar, tae; -

> 'I' aurais ma grammoree.
> Tu aurais ta grammoree.
> Il aurait sa grammoree.
> Nous aurier nos grammoree.
> Vous aurier vos grammoree.
> Ils auraient leurs grammoree' "

"Taisez-vous, taisez-vous!" I exclaimed. "I hate the very soon' o't. But what aboot oor Geometry? – Anither thing I am as much at hame in, as a hen in water. For a long time I couldna understan' the cursed angles ava', but I'm getting' better intil it noo. Ah, but, Pate, look yonder. Yon's what'll dissipate oor thochts o' angles and grammars. See hoo the white crested waves are hurryin' for the shore, roond aboot the Neuk!"

> "Break, break, break,
> On thy cold grey stones, O sea!
> And I would that my tongue could utter
> The thoughts that arise in me:"
> "The zealot, with a blinded will,
> For higher joy than this may pray;
> But give me sight of sea and hill,
> And take your painted dreams away!"

McLaren and I were now within full view of Jovah's Neuk and, in joyful expectation of getting a cool plunge in a short time to refresh us, we reached that rocky promontory, where we sat ourselves down for a wee to admire the surrounding scenery. As the atmosphere was rather thick, we could scarcely discern the Fife coast; but we could see two or three stately ships upon the Firth, with every available canvas expanded on the rigging to catch as much of the too slight breeze as possible; and their sails appeared to be dazzling when the sun's rays fell upon them, but took on a darker hue when his rays were intercepted by a passing cloud. There, too, was a fine-looking pleasure-trip steamer steaming down the Firth, leaving behind a curling column of smoke in the air, and a long track of white foam in the water. Now and then, a white-winged sea-maw was also to be seen skimming over the blue expanse of the rolling deep. But we didn't sit long a-gazing over the sea, as we were over intent on having a dook.

Proceeding a bittie farther east, we found a comfortable and convenient place, where we were soon engaged in divesting ourselves of our clothes. A minute more, and we rushed into the pure and bracing water. Neither of us at that time was able to swim, though we had applied our upmost endeavours in trying to learn that commendable art; but, we amused ourselves by plunging into each successive wave, - for, though there was scarcely a breath of wind, there was a heavy swell on the sea. When we had enjoyed ourselves in this manner for some time, I advanced to meet a huge wave, which was coming rowing in like a little mountain. I dived into it with a shout of glee, but, when I supposed the wave should be past, and made an attempt to rise to my feet, oh, horror of horrors, I couldn't find the bottom! At first I thought another wave had overtaken me; but, when I discovered I was still unable to stand up, I began to struggle with a wild energy, which those only can have who struggle for life, in the hopes that I might be able to bring myself out of my predicament. However, all my efforts proved in vain; and I was compelled to reckon myself a drowning sinner. What a sudden change! A minute before I was shouting in my worldly glee – now, I was nearing the awful brink of Eternity! The queer sensation I felt at that time is utterly beyond my power of description.

I have a recollection of gasping a short but fervent petition to Heaven to be delivered from such an early and watery grave. My prayer was heard and answered. I can mind it well, after being a considerable time, perhaps a few minutes, immersed in the water, I was just feeling as if falling asleep, in short, relapsing into unconsciousness, or, I may say, yielding to the grim king Death, when, to my inexpressible joy, my feet touched the sands, and I immediately raised myself to an upright position, to find myself only waist deep in the water. But at first I felt very weak and sick, until I had vomited some of the water that had almost done for me; then I felt much relieved.

My first impulse, on recovering so far, was to look for my cronie. At a first survey around, me I couldn't see him at all, but soon caught sight of the poor fellow, some fifteen yards from where I stood, convulsively struggling in the water. Whenever I beheld his hapless plight, I instinctively made for the spot, but hadn't advanced many steps, when, to my great delight and satisfaction, he also got to his feet. So far was he gone, however, that the next wave knocked him over. On seeing him recover his feet again, I turned for the shore, shouting on him to come along. Although he slowly moved shoreward, it was the only answer I got, except some gurgling groans. Seeing him in such a state, I straightaway turned to his assistance, took his arm, and led him towards the beach, saying "Come on, Peter; come on, my man, we're safe noo, thank Heaven!" My cronie was much worse than I, as he had probably been longer in the water, and seemed to breathe with some difficulty, until he vomited a large quantity of the water he had imbibed. Thereafter, he revived quickly, and soon comprehended our situation; and we weren't long in getting out of the insidious deep.

But where were we? And where were our clothes? This, for a moment, we couldn't say, as it was quite a different place from that at which we had entered the water. Presently, however, we spotted the place where our clothes lay, about a hundred yards farther west, and there we proceeded without any loss of time. While we were dressing we said little, for both of us, but especially my cronie, were coughing and vomiting rather freely. When we had got our duds all properly adjusted, I seated myself down on the rocks, with an air of complacent satisfaction, saying "Noo, Pate, my mate, we'll transport thae sandwiches elsewhere noo, I guess. Hoo dae ye feel?"

"On, nearly a'richt noo," was the answer: "but I really thocht I was gaun tae turn inside oot. Odds, nouns! Jist a minute or twa ago, I deemed I wad ne'er see you or onybody, again."

"And sae did I, verily. But hoo did we baith get intae sic a dilemma. I canna understan' it at a'!"

"Weel, ye see, Reidie, yon time ye made the dive intae the big wave, I was surprised tae see that ye didna rise again, an' seemed tae struggle for yer feet. Concludin' there was somethin' wrang, I made for ye at ance but, alack, before I could reach ye I was ower my heid. Och, it was awfu' when I thocht I was droonin'! I couldna think on naething but the mither I wad ne'er see again, an' the uncertain gate I wad gang intae the hereafter. But, thank God, that He has seen fit to gie us some time yet for repentance an' remission o' oor sins."

"Aye, aye, Pate lad, ye're richt. Oor experience the day was jist like a glisk intae anither world; I hope it will mak' us a wee thing mair thochtfu' i' the future."

77

"An' better prepared for sic a change as we were amaist undergaun. If it hae been a back-gaun tide, we would undootedly hae been unconscious by this time o' havin' foond a watery grave!"

"Fegs, McLaren, ye're richt again! But hang me gin I can understan' whether we had gane into some deep place, or whether it was a sudden rise o' the tide."

And that same is a mystery to me until this day, and will likely ever be. After doing full justice to the agreeable sandwiches, for which we felt much the better, we were not long in retracing our steps homewards; justly concluding we had enough of the sea for one day. Never were we so glad for seeing the dear familiar faces of Aberlady, and never before did we realise how happy we were, an how sweet is life, as on that day after of our narrow escape from being drowned. Aft, aft, when we two strayed about the sea green, or lay waken in our bed, did we crack about the extraordinary incident of that eventful day; but we never told a half of it to any of our friends, lest they should forbid us to swim again, which would have been a severe sentence on us…The foregoing experience of the dangers of bathing, didn't prevent McLaren and I from indulging in our favourite pastime; for, after it we were oftener in the sea than ever, and struggled hard to swim, which both of us could do little when that summer was done.

Chapter XXVII

As the scene of a good many of the incidents that now fall to be related is Ballencrieff, I will try, before proceeding farther, to describe, as concisely as possible, that not altogether uninteresting place.

Taking the main road from Aberlady to Haddington, you come to a railway brig about two miles from the former, passing through which you will reach two crossroads, where stands Ballencrieff Toll, - for though tolls have long ceased to be in that part of the country, it still retains the name. Now take the left-hand road, and you're 'oot o' the world an' intae Ba'ncrieff', as the saying goes. Although you have just passed a farm called Ballencrieff Mains, yet it isn't generally included in the name Ballencrieff. After leaving the Toll, the next place you come is to the smiddy and smith's house. Here again the road divides, that to the right being the 'coach drive' to the farmhouse. The present farmer has forsaken this road to be used except as a private means of approach to his domicile; but, in the days of which I write, it was the practiced thoroughfare to the Gardens also.

Right opposite the farmhouse on the public road, are the cottars' houses, called 'the Raw', while to the east of it are the Grieve's house, the stables, mill, barn, stack-yard, etc. Ballencrieff farm is the largest in Aberlady parish; and I venture to say is one of the biggest and best in East Lothian. Proceeding along the public road a bit past 'the Raw', or the hind's houses, you come to a road striking off to your right that takes you to the Gardens, thought at the time of these incidents there was no such gate at all. The Gardens, which cover four acres, if I not mistaken, are encompassed by a high dyke. At the east end of the Gardens stands our friend Mr McLaren's house, beside which are the roofless walls of Ballencrieff House, once the seat of Lord Elibank.

This fine mansion was burnt perhaps 12 years ago, and since then has been left deserted of its once gentle occupants, it never having been restored to a habitable condition, but left to the teeth of time and decay to gnaw away at its leisure. It is now the happy and unmolested habitation of numerous jack-daws, starlings, sparrows, and in the summer time, black swallows forbye a couple of bonnie cream-coloured barn owls, which never seem to propagate, as there is never any other than the two ever seen there. One of the first times I visited Ballencrieff I got a real fright from those hoolets. It was a dark winter night, when the garden gate near the house closed with a squeak and clank behind Peter McLaren and I as we made for the house, that an eerie, dismal "Wheest, wheesht!" came from the gloomy ruins. At the sound I abruptly stopped short like a startled hare, thinking it was a suppressed human voice, and that some foul work might be going on. When, however, I was informed by my much amused companion, that it was just the hoolet disturbed by the gate, my fears were immediately dissipated.

If walls had tongues, as they say have ears, I'm certain those old walls of Ballencrieff House could tell many a tale that would make the place far more interesting than anything I've got to say about it can. The view from the top windows of this mansion must have been excellent, especially that to the nor'-west, where a commanding view of the Firth of Forth and the Fife coast could be obtained. Round about the ruins are a number of fine old majestic trees of different kinds, though they got a sorry thinning a many years ago. The field or park which is studded with those trees, is universally knew as Ballencrieff Wilderness, but how it came to be so designated I am quite at a loss to conceive.

Ballencrieff is a very ancient place and name, as I find it mentioned, sometimes along with the 'village o' Gosford', far back in Scottish history. From the Imperial Gazetteer of Scotland I learn that 'a hospital is said to have been founded at Ballencrieff in the 12th century'. At the west end of the Gardens stands what I conjecture to be that very hospital, but having undergone a good deal of alteration and repair from time to time. It has been converted into byres, hen-house, hay-loft, etc., which in the wing of the building lives the body whose occupation it is 'tae mind the fowls an' the kye'. An old stone above the door of Mr McLaren's house, which was found about the place when the house was in course of erection, bears, along with some other sculpture-work, the date 1286. The word "time" is also plainly seen on it, though the word preceding that is altogether defaced, except the last letter, which is an 'm' or a 'w'. I don't mind which. Near the old hospital, at the west end of the Gardens, are the stables, barn, etc., that go along with said Gardens, and land, while at the nor'-west corner of the Gardens, stands the ploughman's house. And now I think I have given a faithful though rude sketch of Ballencrieff.

Ever since my father's demise, my mother has let her house in Aberlady for a few months each year to summer visitors. During the period the house is let she stays at Ballencrieff. The first time she had occasion to spend the summer there, my grandmother and I were along with her; and that gave me an opportunity of being still more than ever aside my inseparable cronie, Peter McLaren. We never tired of playing pranks and making adventures; but most of our hairum-skairum on-goings about this time I have forgotten – the following being exceptions.

One night, when we had won up from the school, and had demolished some supper, the two of us went to the ruins, there expecting to 'find mischief still for idle hands to do' In the ground flat of the old domicile are some dark awesome cells, out of one of which we rolled a big round stone with a hole in the centre of it, which we determined to blast. We soon procured some gun-powder, and a bit of fuse, and some matches; we filled the hole nearly full with the first, laid the fuse to it, and to the end applied a lighted match. This done, we retreated to a respectable distance, there to watch the result of our attempt at blasting. In a jiffy the powder got ignited, and, exploding burst the stone in pieces, a lump of which shot over close to where we stood. After examining the several pieces of stone, we climbed up a projecting and broken-down partition into one of the rooms of the second flat. When we had made an exploration through this and the adjoining apartment, we made for the stair situated about the middle of the mansion, one of those cork-screw round about kinds, with stone steps. As we bounded up that flight of steps as lithe as a couple of hares we were immediately on the top of the ruins.

Here we sat for a twinkling to admire the setting sun, as it imbued the filmy clouds away in the nor'-west with bright and diverse hues. But we couldn't settle long out of mischief, so we were soon employed in throwing stones at holes, out of which we observed bits of sticks and straws protruding, and where, of course, we concluded there was sure to be a jack-daw's nest. Predictably, my cronie, McLaren, proposed to shove a big stone, that was lying nearly loose on the top of the wall at our sides, down the stair. Without thinking on the consequences, we put forth our combined pith to dislodge this stone from its place, and precipitate it onto the flight of steps. So far we succeeded; but, alas, as it tumbled on the stair, great was our consternation when, instead of rolling down the stair, as we had anticipated, it brought down everything in its fall! The top steps on which we stood had fallen to the bottom, but there were still a number left, though these were all more or less broken. Here, we thought, was a fine kettle of fish, as we stood glowering down confounded at the devastation caused by our rash act. Nevertheless we didn't linger long there, but made an attempt, which seemed feasible, to win down from our exalted position. We reached the bottom of the staircase in safety, though not without some difficulty, and soon thereafter departed the ruins.

Chapter XXVII

One Saturday, not long after the down-fall of the stair in old Ballencrieff House, we, Peter McLaren and I, had been over at the loch in the south side of the Wilderness, trying to have a sail on a raft which we had constructed from wood and rushes, and had just reached the house, but over soon for dinner, when we determined to pay another visit to the ruins during the interval. We soon climbed up onto the second flat, and directly made for the dilapidated staircase.

"I hae tae get up tae the top o' that bloomin' stair ance mair!" exclaimed my venturesome cronie, and there and then began to ascend, on all fours, of course. Although I remonstrated at first on the plea of it being a very dangerous thing to attempt, seeing my chum was already a good way up, and quite indifferent to my reasoning, I ultimately followed his example. Before I was much more than half way up, Peter had reached the tap, and was now in the act of descending, so I proposed to go no further. McLaren, being and artful climber, was aside me in a jiffy; and, as we both stood on the same half-step, that had been left projecting out of the wall, we felt it go way, and simultaneously sprung into a closet off the staircase, close to which, by good luck, we chanced to be. This movement was neither superfluous nor a bit over soon, for, at the same time we landed safely in the closet, we heard a rumbling crash, the meaning of which we didn't need to be told. Looking down the place where there was once a flight of steps, it appeared just like an empty draw well, or the inside of a short, wide chimney. The few half-broken steps that had been left from the first down-fall of the stair were now mingled with the rest in a rude heap at the bottom. This made the destruction of the old stair complete; and moreover, it cut off the slender means of descent which a minute previous was in our grasp. Although our height above the floor of the second floor wasn't very great, still to have dreeped would have been very sore to our limbs.

"Unco near, ne'er killed a man", was my cronie's laconic observation, on recognizing our narrow escape.

"Aye!" I returned; "but we're in a fix yet, forsooth. Hoo are we tae win doon?"

"Oh, ne'er fash yer thoom on that heid. Hey! H-e-y!"

friends suggested that I should finish my education elsewhere, but at my earnest solicitation it was agreed instead to look out for a suitable situation for me, as I was now thirteen years old, and an unusually big fellow for my age. Oh! What unbounded rapture I felt at the glorious ought of being entirely free from school laws and lessons for ever. For ever! It was as if I had been transported into a different world altogether.

Some who may chance to peruse those pages, will probably aver, that now, with my better experience in the world's cares and troubles, I see the folly of my earlier sentiments, and wish my school-days back again; but, no! I have done many a sore day's work, and taken a good deal of vexation along with the sad work, since then, but I always consider it a glorious privilege to be able to work, the harder it is the more satisfaction and enjoyment one has when seated down to partake of his daily bread; and I have never entertained, nor will I entertain, the slightest regret that my compulsory education is for ever past. No, I would decidedly prefer to toil with aching limbs, and mind harassed with those cares that are to be encountered at each occupation, than sit cowering in a desk, like a moose in the paw of a lion, fearing to make the least movement, chilled to the heart at the sound of the approaching footstep of a dour, wrathful, and overbearing 'dominie', and compelled, at least expected, to do things that are utterly beyond your capabilities. Yet such is, I must allow, a good preliminary discipline for the 'after battle' of life.

Now that I was altogether done with the school, I was very high and boastful among my cronies, an ever delighted in alluding to the way, in which I quit it. A few days, perhaps one or two weeks, "wing'd there way wi' pleasure' while I still waited at home on the out-look for a job, while working in the garden, or daundering about at leisure.

Aberlady's not a business place at all, and holds out very little choice of employment. Indeed, it's very difficult for one to obtain a job there of whatever kind; therefore, it was readily proposed that I should go to learn some business in Edinburgh. Nevertheless, I didn't relish that idea, and protested so strongly against it, that I was eventually allowed to take an employment in the gardening vocation offered me by our Ballencrieff friend, Mr McLaren. My taste and inclination went a good deal in that direction; and, as my mother argued in my favour, I wouldn't be any the worse for a year's outside work at any rate, as it would better develop my bodily structure (for I had grown a long, tanker-backed laddie of above five feet and a half), and help to establish a strong and healthy constitution.

Chapter XXX

Having in my younger days intently and tentily watched my father when he worked in the garden, and having for years past worked a good deal at such work myself, it was with great facility that I now got initiated into the general round of work in Ballencrieff Gardens. Our regular hours of labour were from six o'clock in the morning till six at night, with two hours (from eleven to one) for dinner, but in the short days, of course, we started with the dawning and stopped with the gloaming, while then our dinner time was considerably curtailed; and, on the other hand, in the summer time, especially on market nights, our hours were often protracted. Mr McLaren kept no regular gardeners, those who worked to him in the garden and fields being what are designated 'gairden labourers'. Forbye the ploughman, Bob Hume mentioned earlier, Jimmie Kellie, Barney Reynolds, and Frank Tipney, an Irishman from the old Isle 'whaur the grass grows green', Jimmie Kellie son of the first-named, a laddie about my own age, the two women who lived in the part of the old hospital aside the fowls and kye, Mennie Park (somehow related, it was said, to the great Mungo), and her auntie, Agnes Muirhead, two spinsters, as hired hands, while others were employed as the work and throng demanded. I generally had other jobs about the garden by myself, but occasionally, according to circumstances, I was located aside some or other of the above-mentioned.

The work of a gardener, as anybody may suppose, is very diversified or varied, new jobs coming continually with the ever changing seasons; and the principle work when I went to Ballencrieff – being in the month of March, if I rightly remember – was the planting and sowing of the various seeds for summer propagation and reproduction; while it fell on me as part of my wider duties to water the plants in the vinery and pots each alternate night.

Thus, I got contentedly settled down to the healthy and interesting, though far from lucrative (as far as common journeymen are concerned) occupation of a gardener – the occupation, by the way, of our first parent, Adam.

Forbye any visits down to my native Aberlady each Saturday night, I was often down through the week, too, - to see the lassies, do I hear you say? Well, so my Ballencrieff friends insinuated, nay, positively, declared; but whether they were right or wrong I won't say – it's all a matter of moonshine now. On the nights I didn't go down to Aberlady I usually busied myself in making useful little fancy baskets, to which job I had taken a great liking; or killed time by daundering about the garden with the gun in my oxter, prepared to discharge its contents at any cushie or such like that, unluckily for them, might happen to come within reach of the little pellets. But, with the exception of taking a hurried glimpse at a local newspaper, maybe once a week, I never read, ocht, not even the Good Book –

shame to tell – except in the Kirk - and as for writing, I can almost say that the only time I had a pen in my hand during my sojourn at Ballencrieff, was one day when old Mrs McLaren of Darnhall put writing materials down before me, and actually wouldn't leall me till she's seen me start an epistle to her youngest son, my absent cronie, Peter. Such was my aversion to reading and writing, which had been so obnoxious to my taste while at school, and such is the way in which I showed my thankfulness in being quit of them.

I wasn't long in becoming quite at home in my new abode (not altogether new), and I soon began to be well acquainted with the different folk about. One day, not long after my introduction to this new sphere of life, I had an opportunity of getting to know the dispositions and peculiarities of some of my neighbours. The day was very stormy and wet, so that outside work had, for the time, to be suspended. I got a job in the vinery to prick out lobelia into boxes; while, in the same place, Jamie Kellie and Barney Reynolds were busy cutting seed potatoes for planting, and Agnes Muirhead was rubbing and blowing away at some kail seed. As for the rest of the workers, Bob Hume had some work to do about the stables, Mennie Park had her fowls and kye to look after, young James Kellie 'wisna oot', and Frank Tipney, who had just been recently married (not for the first time), took the opportunity of the excuse afforded him by the state of the weather, to stay at home in the society of his new bride. The three first-named and myself soon got on to a crack, as we pursued our several tasks in the vinery.

"An' hoo dae ye like tae be a gairdener, Jack?" asked Jamie Kellie.

"Oh, fine." I briefly replied.

"An', noo, that's richt! An' ye like tae live at Ballencrieff?"

"Oh aye! Weel eneuch."

"Oy!" said Barney Reynolds, "but there's nae lassies for him here, though. Sure, I guess he'll be missing some o' his Aberlady swatehearts!"

"What's that ye're talking o' Barney?" returned Kellie. "Man, he's doon at the village amaist every nicht. Dae ye think twa miles will keep Jack separate frae the dear purty colleens?"

"Oh, oy!" said Barney. An' that's the way the wind blows is it? Shure an' I moight have thought so.

"Humph – 'deed!" put in Agnes Muirhead, "I dinna think Johnnie'll fash his heid wi' the lassies. He gangs doon tae Aberlady to see his mammy."

"Ye're richt, Agnes", I hastily tried to affirm.

"Don't decaive yerself, my woman", retorted Kellie. – "But, be my sowl! Did yis ever see a praitie like that, Barney? Sure, I've looked at it all over and over, and St Patrick scourge me if I can find any other than the one eye!"

"That ane surely cam' frae Ireland, Kellie?" Agnes suggested, with a slight contortion of her toothless jaws, and a suggestive smile towards me.

"Nay, by the pipers!" exclaimed Barney, "let me see it? – So it is, man. But did I think for a moment that the tattie came from ould Ireland, I would have Jack there plant it in a six-inch flower-pot, and why, woman, it moight grow a purty shamrock!"

"That wad be a new fangled metamorphosis," I ventured to remark. "But, I say, Barney," I added, "Ireland's a rare country for tatties, isna it?"

"Oy, be jabbers it's a moighty good land for everything – except landlords! – Yiss, Jack, and there's heaps of fun for a fellow yonder. They foight there by the square yard. And it's a free country, too – at ony rate the pigs enjoy a good amount of freedom, and that they do. Ah, sure! When I think of the dear old land that I may never see more:

> "O steer my bark to Erin's isle,
> For Erin is my home!"

Ah, if they'd only let a fellow work over yonder, I moight very near think of returning to the Green Isle again. Oy! And that puts me in moind of what Mickie Flynn said, when asked if he has ever seen the Queen. 'Did I ever see the Queen?' says he 'No, I never saw the Queen; but my uncle once very near saw the Duke of York!'"

"Eh, ye're an awfu' man, Barney", exclaimed Agnes, While, almost spontaneously, Kellie began to sing –

> "Impudent Barney, nane of your blarney,
> Impudent Barney O'Hare"

"Ah, but", Barney resumed, with a self-satisfied smile, "I heard a rich one the other day. You know ould Pat O'Reilly who naps stones along at Mungoswells there? Well, one day lately while he was working away yonder beside his heap of road-metal, a man came forward to him, and suspecting by his general appearance that he was an Irishman, said, 'Will you tell me the road to Drem, Pat!" Pat looked

90

up from his work, and taking a survey of the stranger, replied. "Well, now," said he, "how did you know my name was Pat?" "Oh," says the man, "I guessed it". "Sure then," says Pat, "seeing as you're such a moighty good guesser, you can guess the road to Drem, too, - and be off wid yis!"

After a short pause in our crack, Kellie exclaimed as he glowered up at the water pouring down the sashes – "Man alive, how it rains! Did yis ever see the like of it? It's coming down in bucketfuls."

"Oh oy!" said Barney, "it will do a heap o' good, anyhow, and that it will. But, I say, Agnes, what was up with you and Kirsty Mucklenackit yesterday?"

"Ou, naething parteeclar," was Agnes's raith, dreich response. "Only, that she threepit doon my throat that I'd gien her twa rotten eggs amang half a dizzen she bocht on Monday. When she cam' for them, d'ye see, Mennie wisna in, sae I jist gien her half a dizzen o' them that were lyin' on the shelf in the hall. Weel, what d'ye think, in comes Kirsty yesterday rampagin' up to tae the 'toon' (for such the old hospital, etc., is termed by some) "and I forgaithered wi' her in the coort yonder, when, ma conscience! As Bailie Nicol Jarvie would say, she 'yokit to me like a randy vixen'. Kirsty says, says she, 'What kin' o' eggs were thae you gien me yesterday?' says she. 'Twa o' them were rotten,' says she, 'and set up a smell i' the hoose, as gin there were s stinkin' brock in't' says she. 'An' gin I didna hear tell o'it frae my man, my sang!' says she, 'I ken best.' I says, says I, 'Weel,' says I, 'I dinna ken hoo that could be,' says I; 'for I jist took them frae among the lave in the hall,' says I. 'But,' says I, 'it's nae use,' says I, 'we'll see what Mennie says aboot it, and gin it's really a fac' says I, 'that ye gat twa rotten anes (though I dinna see hoo it could be),' says I, 'then' says I, I've nae doot' says I, 'but that ye'll get twa guid anes for them. Dinna think,' says I, 'that I was wantin' tae cheat ye – certainly na!' says I."

"Sae, you see, when I tauld Mennie aboot the mistak', she couldna understaun' it aither; but, seein' Kirsty threepit that she was telling the truth, she gat anither twa eggs for them she declared were rotten. But, you ken the woman, an' I daursay ye'll jalouse as weel as me it seems an unco clever dodge on her pairt tae get the twa eggs for naething. Gin she was speakin' the truth, hooever, twa o' the nest eggs maun hae gotten mixed up wi the lave, somehoo or ither. Eh! Bye the bye, Johnnie, that minds me tae tell ye that Mennie wants ye tae spiel up tae the auld lum in the hay-laft the nicht, - ye're a young soople fella, ye ken, - an' see gin that hen has laid ony mair eggs there."

"Oh, aye, Agnes," I replied, "that's a rare job for the likes o' me!"

In such a way, then, the crack, with slight interruptions, was sustained until the six o'clock train flying past announced the approach of the 'lowsing time'.

Chapter XXXI

The little bursting buds of spring had developed into the bonnie fresh green leaves and scented blossom of early summer; and they, in turn, had given place to the more abundant, but less glossy and pure, foliage and luscious fruit of the later part of summer. The birds, which, at the time I went to Ballencrieff, had scarcely commenced to build their nests, were now tempting and teaching their full-feathered off-spring to rise more buoyantly on their as yet inexperienced wings; while later birds might still be seen carrying mouthfuls of food to the very ready mouths of their downy progeny. The flowers throughout the garden were now just about their bonniest, and made a fine relief to the more sombre and less beautiful hues of fruit trees, shrubs, vegetables and what not. The strawberries were in their very prime; and some of the earliest gooseberries were just ripening; though the earliest apples were yet some weeks from maturity. The kidney potatoes on the borders were also ready for lifting; - and just, in short, our very busiest time in the garden had now begun in earnest.

The van was in at the Edinburgh market three times a week. The days on which it went were Tuesday, Thursday and Saturday; but the van having to start on the road at, or about, midnight, the stuff, of course, had all to be prepared and packed in the night previous, so that our busiest days were Monday, Wednesday, and Friday.

As the fruit season approached the garden became quite overrun with birds of diverse kinds; those most injurious to the fruit being the blackies and mavises, and sometimes cushies, - but these last seldom alighted in the garden if anybody was in it, and though we tried many a stratagem to get a shot at them, they generally proved over fly for us. At dinner time and at night, it was my practice to scour the garden with the gun, in order to scare away the birds, and make examples of some of them. This led me to enjoy shooting; and I sometimes ventured outwith the boundaries of the garden in pursuit of cushies and crows, and sometimes game. At this time, there was a young fellow, considerably older than myself, however, called Jack Thomson, from Ballencrieff Mains, working to Mr McLaren, who, being a keen hand at the gun, generally joined me in hunting the blackies, felties, and mavises out of the garden.

One day, after having hurried over with my dinner, I hastened out to the garden, ettling to have a shot, and just met Jack Thomson coming up 'the middle walk'.

92

"There it is! There it is!" he exclaimed.

In a twinkling I had shouldered the fowling piece, by which time the water-hen had emerged from among the rushes, and was now making its way on its rather incompetent wings over the hedge on the far away side of Jack Thomson, at an almost equal elevation with his head. So keen was I to shoot the frightened and innocent bird, that even at this critical point, without anticipating the possible consequences, I let go one of the barrels at it, and the bird dropped over the hedge. Almost paralysed with fright, Thomson stood glowering at me as if I'd lost my reason 'stoup and roup'; while I, myself, could scarcely believe what I'd done.

"Confound it! Jack," I began to explain and apologize, "the shot was aff afore I kent whit I was daein'. But I'm doonricht gled that you're nane the waur for my reckless haste in shuitin', when the object o' my aim was sae near yer heid."

"An' dae ye no think," he answered, "that I'm e'en mair gled than yersel'? Fegs, John, I got an unco fleg, though. I wasna shure for a blink whether I was deid or livin' whether my heid or feet were upmaist. I'm thinking that was e'en a narrower escape than what ye had through my carelessness."

"Aye," I returned, "they were baith near eneuch; but it was mair through sheer thochtlessness on my pairt, an' mair through accident on yours. But what o' the water-hen noo?"

"I'm thinkin', my lad, that ye will ne'er see hint nor hair o' it again."

"Fient a bit o' that! I'm amaist certain that it fell ower the hedge, if no a' thegither killed, woundit at the least."

Without any more words or waste of time, the two of us proceeded to look for the water-hen, or coot. We found it quite dead, behind the hedge as I had expected; and, contented with our small success, we thereafter made our way home, I taking the waterhen with me. It was a very bonnie bird, and being very perfect, no perceptible marks of the shot about it, I got it stuffed, in which condition it still stands on its long feet in the house.

It may not be altogether out of place for me here to depict the scene presented, as it is stamped on my recollection, at the felling of one of the biggest trees in Ballencrieff Wilderness.

There then it stands, and has stood for a good many centuries – a mighty beech, whose spreading branches extend far and wide, and below their kindly shade we now feel as if the sun had set. Two or three crows' nests are to be spotted among its myriad smaller branches near the top; but they shall be the last, - though, good faith they are not the first that have been built there!....And this grand old majestic tree, which we had admired, both while it was covered with its glossy leaves and haunted by that richest of our woodland warblers the sweet voiced "mellow mavis, that hails the nicht fa'"and while its graceful branches were bending below the load of the winter's snow, is now doomed to be cut down, and laid on the turf that its branches have so long shaded. Ah, if Shakespeare's figure of speech that we "find tongues in trees" were literally true, how our ears might be charmed by the fascinating tales that this old beech could tell of other days. Perhaps it might tell of doughty and heroic deeds, bloody encounters, or thrilling tournaments, which it had witnessed; or, perhaps it might tell how some of the fair daughters of yon old ruined castle would come here to meet their gallant knights or gentle lovers.

But, lo! There the broad woodmen have begun their work. The big heavy axe is dexterously applied to the aged trunk of the tree, as the men dress it round the bottom, previous to it being sawn. See how the axes flash and cut into the sappy wood at each muscular stroke! And, see how the showers of chips are flying around! – The tree is now ready for the big cross-cut saw, and two of the men have begun to saw it at the side desired. As the incision gets deeper, the working in of the saw consequently becomes stiffer, so two other men are put to it; and, shortly afterwards, still two other men are added, so that there are now six men, three on each side, cutting away with the big saw at the majestic looking beech, which has braved the storms of so many winters, but is now, alas, destined to fall at the hands of ruthless Man. The trunk is cut more nor half through, and iron wedges are driven in at the mouth at the cut, for the double purpose of making the saw work easier, and making the tree incline to the side required.

The teeth of the saw have now made their way to within nine inches of being completely through the trunk. Still the old beech stands, as if determined to keep its hold on old Mother Earth as long as possible; but the men are now ready to stand clear whenever any symptoms are shown of the tree yielding. Hark! That crackling, rending sound is it's parting groan! And, as I stand beholding the huge tree swaying earthward, I can scarcely believe that it is it that is tumbling and not I. A moment more, and there's a crash like the loudest thunder; the earth shakes as if there was an earthquake; and see, the felled tree is lying on the sward, with a good many of its aged limbs broken, some of which are stuck many feet into the ground; while the crows' nests have got an unmerciful whumbling.

It is wonderful what an amount of ground the felled tree covers, and what a number of cart-loads of wood can be had here, independent of the sousy trunk and larger branches. The woodmen have now their job before them to 'limb' this fine specimen of a good old beech. In a few days it will be transported to the wood yard; but 'the place that once knew it, and knows it no more' will long appear a pitiful blank to the admirers of Nature.

I mind, one day, when I paid the woodmen my practiced daily visit, I found Jack Thomson and Bill Hay, another acquaintance of mine, busy in smoking a bees' nest in a hole in an elm tree they had just felled. After the bees were smoked out, an entrance was effected into their well-guarded byke, or nest, when it was discovered that the industrious little insects had left us a welcome legacy of honeycomb, in very fair perfection. Some two or three fugitive bees buzzing angrily around our heads made us desist for a short time from further aggression to their already despoiled castle; and that puts me in mind of what a poetic friend says, in an address to a kindred insect, the more ruthless wasp, -

> "When roon' their heids ye loup an' dance,
> Tae guard a thrust o' yer wee lance
> Is past their pooer-
> Aneath a bush, their only chance,
> Frae ye tae cover.
> An' yet it seems sae droll a sicht
> Tae see a man, sax feet in heicht,
> Hidin' frae thee for very fricht –
> Thou tiny wasp,
> Wha could yer lives by thousands blicht
> Wi' a'e fell grasp."

However, it was the more gentle bees we had to deal with, so instead of hiding we stood stock still until they had fled the spot, when we at once assailed their byke, and laid siege to the honey, the men pitting their share of it into their pitchers, after sampling its agreeable flavour. Moreover, they gave me, out of compliment, a good big daud of the comb away with me, which I ate with great relish, but felt very sick after this unaccustomed feast.

It wasn't each day, however, that we got a bees' byke to plunder, and we generally had to content ourselves with getting some suitable branch, wherewith to make a rung or walking-stick.

Chapter XXXIII

I stated in the preceding chapter that I had something to relate about the gaffer of the woodmen, Dauvit Bell, or as he was generally termed among us, 'Old Jethart', after his native town, and so it behoves me now, before proceeding further, to say forth my say. When this worthy first visited Ballencrieff to take a survey of the trees with the fatal stamp or death-warrant upon them (in the shape of a peeled bit of the trunk with the letter "D" impressed thereon), and make arrangements with Mr Dyer about the cutting down of the said trees, he thereafter accepted Mr McLaren's offer to give him a room in the house, and also his board, when he came to accomplish, or, rather, execute his contract, but on what particular conditions I scarcely recollect. In due time our lodger arrived with his bag and baggage; and he there and then took up his abode in the room allotted him, that being what we called the store-room, a spacious apartment upstairs.

From the very first we considered Mr Dauvit Bell as a very eccentric character; but not till the very last did we see him in what were perhaps his true colours. Odds, nouns, but he was a droll looking shaver! Of an average stature, he was extremely bandy-legged, so much so, that standing with his heels close together, a dog might have had no difficulty in jumping through between his knees. He was very thick around the haunches, but not so around the shoulders, which had a most decided slope, and were very bent forward, forbye one of them being lower and apparently weaker than the other, which made him walk with his head slightly to one side, and the arm pendant on the weaker shoulder hanging quietly by his side, while the other did all the swinging. His face a peculiar expression, which was rather difficult to understand, and quite beyond my power of description. If I mind right, he had a short birsy moustache and whiskers, but no beard. And lastly, he wore a brown wig, not that he possessed no hair on his pow-like 'Uncle Ned', for he has as much as the generality of old men – which I should know, seeing as I got the job to cut it one night, and all the time of my inexperienced operations he was comfortably sleeping – but 'jist tae mak' him look younger'.

That, then, is a rude description of the outward man, but the inward man, or his character, we couldn't comprehend at all, far less decipher it. He pretended – for I'm sure it must have been pretence – to be very pious; and we in the kitchen below could hear him repeat long, and seemingly earnest, prayers almost each night. He took very good care for a long time that his words and actions didn't belie his aspirations to piety; and we were almost led to believe that he was a really good man. Nonetheless, during his stay at Ballencrieff, which extended over a month or two, he only once could be persuaded to go to the Kirk, and that was one night when he accompanied me to the U.P. Kirk in Aberlady, where he slept during the whole of the sermon, but, notwithstanding all that, went up to the house and told them, when asked, that he had liked the preacher's discourse very well. To his credit, however, I must say that he lived very thriftily, soberly, and quietly, and was always civil and cracky to all and sundry about the place.

But, all this kenspeckle old body's eccentric actions and droll sayings I must skip over, and task my memory to indict, and my pen to depict, the lively, and to me, amusing, scene he caused on the occasion of his leaving Ballencrieff.

It was one Friday night, an extraordinary busy night with us, and we sat preparing flowers for the Edinburgh market, the bright lamp – for it was already very late – shedding its rays over the big kitchen table, which was heaped with a motley collection of various flowers, all lying awaiting to be composed into bunches and bouquets. At the toe end of the table was seated 'the master', as he was called, myself at the other end, and Mrs Mc----- at the side, the three of us swiftly, but generally, silently, shaping the flowers before us into saleable bouquets; while my mother occupied a seat at a side table, and busied herself in putting a large collection of rose buds into little bunches and "buttonholes". Reclining on the sofa was 'Old Jethart', *alias* Mr Dauvit Bell, a seemingly interested spectator of the busy scene; and over at the ingle neuk sat the servant lass nursing the bairn. Before the cheery fire in happy slumber lay the retriever dog Rosa, with the cat, also in the Land of Nod, snugly nestling in the small of its body in front of its hind legs. Both Rosa and Boldrons are now no more; but the dog, a favourite beastie with everyone about the place, except Old Jethart, who was always very suspicious of it, was the sorest lamented. It almost answered exactly to Burn's description of the dog Luath: -

> "She was a gash an' faithfu' tyke,
> As ever lap ower sheuch or dyke,
> Her honest, sonsy, braw sout face,
> Aye gat her freen's in ilka place;
>
> Her breast was white, her towsy back
> Weel clad wi' coat o' glossy black;
> Her gawky tail, wi' upward curl,
> Hung ower her hurdies wi' a swirl."

But one day she disappeared, and though we for two or three days after were still expecting to see her return, she never came back again; and so we concluded that the unfortunate animal had met with some accident – very probably shot.

As Dauvit Bell had resolved to set off on the following day (Saturday) before 'the master' would be home from the market, the latter now sat in momentary expectation of the old carle coming to some sort of reckoning about the 'lawing'. He had promised the woodman the loan of the horse and cart, which he had ordered one of the men to have ready to drive along to the station with the body's tools, etc., himself and all, so that each thing was prepared for his departure. But the old man seemed very averse indeed to come to a reckoning with Mr McLaren; in order to elude it, he always took the other turn outside, expecting to find the latter in bed when he returned. But that 'cock wouldna ficht'; and so, impatient of waiting, 'the master' found it necessary at last to broach the subject himself when an opportunity occurred.

At first our acquaintance appeared very gracious; but his unwillingness to pay down the reckoning had become apparent in a short time, and an altercation immediately ensued. The argument soon became fast and furious; but, at this period, seeing I wasn't concerned in the affair, the bouquets finished, and my presence not required, I went my way up the stair to my bed, leaving the Heelander and the Borderer to debate the subject as they liked. No sooner, however, had I got myself divested of clothes and comfortably lain down, than I heard some screams from the females, and some other indefinable commotion down-stairs, which at once aroused my curiosity and anxiety. In a jiffy, I banged up out of my bed, hastily jumped into my trousers, and, buttoning them on the way, made a precipitate adjournment to the kitchen below. The first thing that met my eager gaze when I thrust open the door was Jethart slowly wiping off some water that was trickling down his pitifully melancholy face, and exclaiming in most ludicrous tones – "Ech, howe, mey! This is awfu' maister. What are ye gangin' tae dae til me noo?"

McLaren, while sprinkling some water out of a jug on the flowers as he packed them into the hampers, had been so exasperated with the woodman's conduct, and "line of defence" as it were, that he had thrown the contents of the jug in the old dotard's face, wherefore the upshot.

"Noo," said McLaren, not in a mood to be trifled with, "look ye here, ye auld humbug! You've dune me oot o' my sleep this nicht, an' it's time I was gettin' ready tae start; but, gin ye winna pay your lawin' at ance, I'll keep your tools till ye come to an honest reckonin'."

So, saying, he went out to the stick-house, at or near the back door, where wood, coals, etc. were kept, and where the woodman had liberty to house his tools – in order to lock the door of it and retain the key; but he found the door already locked and the key gone. Returning into the kitchen, now roused to a funk, and knowing that none of us had locked the stick-house door, he at once confronted Dauvit Bell, and sternly demanded the key of him.

"Noo maister," answered the now rather agitated woodman, "I haena gat the key."

"Whaur is it then? Ye had it last."

"Ech, howe, mey! Is it no in the lock?"

"No; an' ye ken that well eneuch. Again I say, where's the key?"

102

"I haena gat it, I tell ee; but its aiblins alow the door. Noo maister," added Jethart, as McLaren seized him by the arm "are ye gangin' tae murder mey? Ech, howe, mey!"

"Aye, I'll murder ye, ye auld donnert, cheating, hypocritical, confounded blackguard! But ye'll come and show me where that key is. Johnny, bring a candle, man, or we look for it, gin he hasna got it."

I soon procured a candle, and lit it, while Mrs McLaren and my mother entreated Mr McLaren to let the old man be; but he told them he knew what he was doing, and dragged old Jethart to the stick-house, whither I followed with the lit candle, trembling, half with cold (for I was partially naked), and half with excitement. The Jedburgh worthy told us that the key first was in one place, then was another, and then was in another, but each successive time he lied, and, so, we were obliged to give up the fruitless search.

McLaren, baffled in this respect, was determined still that he shouldn't get off so easy; so he took him up to his room, into which he unceremoniously locked him, saying he would see what was to be done in the morning...When the wily old dotard was thus shut into his room and his expectations of slipping off scot-free frustrated, he was heard to subside heavily into a chair, with his invariable exclamation, "Ech, howe, mey!"

"Noo, Johnny, lad," said 'the master' when he returned to the kitchen, "this ugly affair has upset oor plans a'thegither, and ye'll need to gang tae the market the nicht, as I'll hae tae bide at hame tae look aifter that rapscallion foxy scoondrel – the starnation foxy scoondrel that he is! – But I'll see an' get in with the first train i' the mornin'."

"Very weel!" was my only reply. I was never very averse to go into the market, now and again. So, after receiving full instructions about the prices of the different things, and the quantity of stuff that had been ordered by his several customers, I hurriedly prepared myself for taking the way. With a hamper of flowers in each arm I left the house for the van-shed about a quarter past twelve o'clock, the usual time for leaving, 'the master' giving me strict injunctions to remember all his directions concerning the fruit, vegetables, flowers, etc., to be disposed of at the Edinburgh market. When I reached the foot of the garden I found Bob, the ploughman and market-man, in the stable harnessing old Tib, one of the horses, in the uncertain light of –

> "the struggling moonbeam's misty light,
> And the lantern dimly burning."

103

"Halloah!" he exclaimed on observing me. "It's ye, is it? Whaur's the maister; is he there?"

"No, he's no comin' in the nicht, and I've tae gang instead."

"Oh, hocky, pocky! – Yet, sma' fry's better than nane; an' they say bad company's better than nane tae, but I dinna ken aboot that. Noo, what is up, in a' the world?"

"Oh, I'll tell ye anon, gin ye gie me less of yer impudence; but I think it's high time we were aff, is it no?"

"Ay, aye! – Come on, Tib! – Gee, gee! – Get oot o' the gait man. Bring the lantern wi' ye, will ye? Wo, wo!"

I took the lantern as requested, having previously laid down the flower hampers at the shed door, and followed Bob and the horse thither, where we yoked the good brown mare into the well-loaded van. Having placed the flower hampers, and also a couple of grape hampers which had been brought down after loading-time, on the top, and water-proof covering thrown over and tied to the sides of the van. Bob now led Tib out of the van-shed into the court or stack-yard, then returned to stick the door, and put the lantern into the stable; while I got myself seated on the right-hand front corner of the van as comfortably as a projecting gallon basket at my back would allow. This done, Bob took his seat on the "near" side of me, and the least touch of the reins made Tib start off at a brisk walking pace, so –

> "Wi' a hi', wo, gee, wo!
> Awa' we gang sae cheery."

It wasn't long before Bob asked the reason of the master not going in as usual that night, and in fact I don't think I could have kept it any longer, it so occupied my mind, so I told him all I had seen and heard, which greatly amused him, and kept him in good trim all that morning. We arrived with the van in Edinburgh a bit before six o'clock a.m. and, after stopping for some time at a fruiterer's shop in Leith Walk, where some peas and flowers had been ordered, we proceeded to the Waverley Market. At this time, the market was just in prospect of being covered in, but had not yet been commenced, so that the gardeners were then exposed to the elements.

The morning that Bob and I alighted there, however, was exceptionally fine; and, after securing our usual stance, which was about the middle of the market, we busied ourselves in unloading the van, - putting the vegetables, fruits, and flowers in tiers upon the causey, of course, showing them off to the best advantage we could. At seven o'clock the gates were opened to the public, who flocked in like a swarm of bees, men and women unceremoniously jostling one another about in the common race to be foremost. There was the fruiterer and greengrocer with a 'shining morning face', and all his business abilities about him; there the hawker and street-vendor with her much basket on her arm, and now telling the party with whom she is at present dealing that she could get stuff of better quality and far cheaper (why does she not, then?), and at last buying a quantity, if any at all, of second-class stuff at the very lowest price to which she can get it; there the lady with her more genteel basket, looking out for some cheap fruit for her preserves; and there the "laddie-da" gent seeking a suitable flower for his button-hole, or the smiling-faced, superlative miss wanting to purchase a bouquet or nose-gay, at least so she says.

Oh! What a crowd of forms rush to my recollection as I think on that scene; but the most conspicuous among them is that of 'Cocoa-nut Tammy', a High Street worthy, who was in daily attendance on the gardeners with his round shoulders, a sprig of heather in his ragged-coat button-hole, and his funny face – which generally had the appearance of soap and water on "high-days and holidays" – peering out below the shadow of a broad-rimmed old felt hat. Tammy could do a wee bit stroke of business in his own unambitious way, and could be serious enough, too, when he liked; but he was generally making rude jokes, or, emitting long harangues, well diversified with bans and oaths, in a comical and good-humoured manner.

In a couple of hours more nor half of the stuff was disposed of; but by this time the throng of the morning was past, so that, to get the remainder of our load sold it was consequently necessary to reduce the prices. It was then that Mr McLaren turned up in the market, having arrived with the first train, and at once began to bargain away about some apples and French beans, with a fruiterer who had just come along with him. You may be sure that at the first favourable opportunity I asked of 'the master', how he had got on with Jethart.

"Oh, the rapscallion!" he replied. "The bird has flown."

"The bird has flown?" I interrogatively repeated.

"Aye, the bird has flown, an' left the nest empty, which I didna reckon upon. Dae ye no understaun'? Weel, when I gaed up tae the storeroom this mornin' tae see what the auld cuif had to sae for himsel', guess my surprise when he wasna tae be foond there. The back window was open, frae whilk I concluded that he maun hae dreepit frae there tae the grund, - a raither desperate action for an auld man like him. The neist thing I did was tae gae tae the stick-hoose, an' there was the key we looked for sae lang last nicht sticking in the lock, an' the wudman's tools still in their place, they bein' ower muckle for the auld carle tae tak' awa' wi' him. I

105

lockit the door, takin' the key wi' me, sae my gentleman can get his tools when he pays me doon what he's owin'.''

Mr McLaren just terminated his explanation in time to attend to a lady who was asking the price of one of the remaining bouquets; while Bob and I turned to discuss, criticise, and wonder at Mr Dauvit Bell's unlooked for course of actions. That afternoon, shortly after Mr McLaren and I had won home, the servant entering the back door brought the intelligence that old Mr Bell was out there wanting to speak to 'the master'. The latter therefore arose from his armchair, and went over to the door; and there was the forester solemnly standing at a safe and respectable distance over in the field at the back of the house.

"Weel?" was his brief salutation. "Are you gangin' tae let me get my tools noo, maister?" said Mr Bell.

"Aye, on condition o' yer clearin' other accounts."

"He, ma conscience! Are ee gangin' tae begin again? Weel, sir, I tell ee what it is; ye've made my airm black an' blue wi' yer violence last nicht, an' I'll jist gang tae Haddington an' lode an action again ee for assault, I wull."

"Ye're welcome," replied the other, returning into the kitchen; while Old Jethart strode away, exclaiming, "Ech, howe, mey!"

That same afternoon, a wee bit later on, Mr McLaren deemed it advisable to go to Haddington himself, and consult a certain lawyer, an acquaintance of his, about this bothersome affair, which was now assuming a rather serious aspect. He there saw his friend all right, described the whole affair to him, put the matter into his hands, and returned home. About half-road between Haddington and Ballencrieff he met none other than the man who was the cause of all this ado slowly plying his way to the county town. Giving the other a very suspicious and not overly confidential look, Old Jethart remarked that he was going to make good his word, and put his case before the court.

"Ye may as weel save yersel' the trouble," answered McLaren, "for I've jist been there afore ye; an' I'm gey shure ye'll mak' naethin' o' it."

"He, ma conscience!" returned the woodman, "ye'll see aboot that," and was very glad to get past.

But this long account of a quite unimportant, and perhaps, to the reader, uninteresting event, I must now cut short, as I fear, I have dwelt over long on it already. We were kept for some time in rueful expectation – but I need not say *we*

106

for *I* was then under age, I think, for such an honour – of having to attend as witnesses at the Sheriff Court at Haddington, However, the parties meant to be represented by the personal pronoun "we" were just as well pleased when the case of Bell v. McLaren was withdrawn. Our old Border friend returned some time after, and came to a kind of settlement, so that he got away his tools alright; and Ballencrieff has never, I think, had the pleasure of seeing him since then.

Chapter XXXIV

"The autumn mune was shinin' bricht
Ower stibble, lea, an' stook,"

as Mrs McLaren and I left the house with a couple of flower hampers each, one Friday night, or Saturday morning, rather, - for it was after midnight, - to go in to the market. We soon reached the stables, where the ploughman, Bob, had the horse already for yoking, and in other five minutes were driving through by Wilson's gay and roughly causeyed stable-court.

We were both seated at the front of the van, 'the master' at the one side and I at the other. Our crack, or conversation, was very limited; for, with the exception of passing some remarks on the weather and crops, generally the most absorbing topic among us, and observing, at times, that some of the things at the top of the van were not very steady, we mutely resigned ourselves to our own wandering thoughts, and, perhaps, our own dreams, for it wasn't unusual for us to take a bit nap on the road. We had passed Standalone, Loch-hill, and Spittal, successfully, and were now being carried through that little, but dense, and at this time of year, the leaves still being on the over-spreading and intertwining branches of the trees, extremely dark wood at the head of the bonnie walk leading from Gosford, called 'The Thornie Lane', at Redhouse. The moon was very well round to the west, her rays being completely excluded (and would have been, at whatever part of the lift she might reign) from that part of the road we were now traversing. A solitary hoolet was piercing the still air with its eerie, weird, midnight screech, as it circled round the ancient ruins of Redhouse.

This ruined castle of Redhouse is one of the oldest mansions, still standing, in East Lothian. It formerly belonged to the Houses of Elibank, but latterly became the property of the more powerful House of Wemyss. It has long been in irreparable ruin, and the side of it next the road, and the gables are now almost wholly covered with ivy; but though slowly 'crumbling to decay', it is rather picturesque and interesting. Well, I had just been about falling asleep as we entered the above-mentioned wood, but the sudden change of scene, the clank of the horse's feet, and the rattle of the wheels then becoming louder, and evoking an audible echo from the ruins, helped to keep me a while longer waken.

Redhouse had been left some thirty yards behind, and I had just got myself placed into as comfortable a position as circumstances wood allow, in order to have a snooze, when our attention was attracted by a group of poachers lying quietly by the road-side. There were six or seven of them, very ruffian looking fellows; and they had guns with them, forbye a number of half-starved looking dogs of various breeds. The men didn't stir until we were two or three yards past them, when some of the group arose, and, as far as we could discern, came up behind the van. Although Mr McLaren was almost certain that the poachers were at the back of the van, it was deemed safest to keep our seats and say nothing. This was very trying, to think that our goods were very probably being stolen wholesale, and we were sitting there inactive, not doing a finger's turn to try and save them; but, what could we two have done against that lawless group with their dogs and guns? Most likely if we had interrupted them, they might have come to violence and, in that case, we assuredly would have got the worst of it, so we let them be.

When we reached the first rail-way crossing after passing Longniddry we jumped off our seats, (it was our practice at any rate to walk between this and the next crossing), and immediately went to the back of the van to ascertain if the poachers had really taken anything. Our suspicions were not groundless, for we soon discovered that two or three gallon-baskets of fruit – I don't exactly mind the particular kind – had disappeared. On passing by, McLaren told the old man who kept the gates about the taking of the fruit, and how he suspected it had been done. The gate man, in response, said he had seen some very suspicious looking fellows pass that way not very long before; and then he began to relate some experiences and adventures he had had with poachers at different times. But as time pressed, and Tib was briskly pacing the road quite Independent of us, we had to leave him in the middle of one of his stories.

We met up on other two market vans when we reached the next railway crossing – they being from Redhouse and the Byres respectively, so that both of them had passed the spot where we had seen the group of poachers. If I mind rightly, the Byres van had met with the same fate as ours, but the driver had been asleep while passing that gate, so that he didn't see the men; but the man from Redhouse had observed them, although he had got by them scatheless. When we returned from the market that afternoon we found the road between Harelaw and Redhouse partially strewn with the stolen fruit; and, after a good deal of searching, we discovered the empty baskets behind the hedge that fenced the road. The police were informed of the affair, but, as was expected, no inkling of the men was ever obtained. However, that was the first, and as far as known, it is the only time that

108

anything of the kind has happened, and, though it was nothing very serious, it is to be hoped it will be the last.

Thus passed my days and nights at Ballencrieff, and I still continued to go to Aberlady on the Sundays, and occasionally through the week after supper-time. The fruit of the garden was now almost done, the leaves were beginning to fall, the corn was all safely led in to the stack-yard, and bleak-faced Hallowmas was once more fast approaching. We were now joyfully looking forward to our participation in the annual 'jovial, ranting kirn'. To me, especially, the kirn was a grand spree, and very much longed for, as I was then an enthusiast in the art of dancing, and had just lately learned how to move about on the "light fantastic toe". Once in the decorated barn, which served as a ballroom, and with 'rural life o' every station'' around me, each one seemingly more blythesome than another, I felt a good deal of the spirit of the "grey-haired father", whom the poet says: -

"Dance, my children, lads and lassies;
    cut 'n' shuffle, toes and heels; -
Piper, roar from every chanter,
    Hurricanes of Highland reels!

Make the old barn shake with laughter;
    Beat its floorin' like a drum,
Batter it with Tullochgorum,
    Till the storm without is dumb!

Sweep in circles like a whirlwind;
    Flit about like meteors glancing;
Cack your fingers, shout for gladness,
    Think of nothing but of dancing."

But I won't go any further in writing about the kirn here, as I have attempted, with not much success, likely, to describe that rural festival – which I'm sad to think is gradually being done away with – in my 'Rhymes'.

The kirn past, the 'Dark Howe o' the Year', soon began to dawn upon us, bringing with it the short days and dirty weather; and we had to settle down to the less genial work of the winter time.

Chapter XXXV

The one only general holiday – to the farm folk, at least – in East Lothian is Old Hansel Monday, that is the first Monday after the twelfth of January, the said twelfth being the old New Year's Day. Hansel Monday is held in those rural districts in much the same way as New Year's Day is held in our towns. Currant loaf and whisky are the two principle elements of the day. Then there is the gathering of friends, old acquaintances, and old fellow-workers, who have been separated by the unscrupulous fate which made our own beloved poet sing that 'Man was made to Mourn'.

Who would censure or ridicule the honest, hard-worked rustic, that, after welcoming an old acquaintance that once neighboured him on the hairstrig or used to 'yoke a naig' with him, or held his plough in the next furrow to his, produces, after his blunt but kindly salutation, the black bottle, out of which he fills a perhaps bottomless glass, and presses it on his friend with a daud of currant loaf to cool his 'weeted craig'? Who knows if they should ever meet again? And, even if they should, what hardships they must endure, and how many long days must they toil before the next Hansel Monday or Hiring Friday. Nay, I think they may even be excused if, under such circumstances, they forget for a while to 'be temperate in all things', and in their boisterous glee imbibe over much of the intoxicating liquor.

I shall here tell how I spent this Hansel Monday in Aberlady; and in dealing with the different events of the day, it will suffice to give the reader an inkling of how that holiday is observed in most of the rural clachans throughout the county. But the reader, like myself, may know well enough by experience what kind of day it is. Well, if so be the case, my humble description of it may bring home to his mind some dear recollections that may, perhaps, afford him a minute's joy.

The two principal holidays in Aberlady, as I've said before, are Old Hansel Monday, and the "Race"; but the latter is confined to the village, while the other universal throughout the district. But to the point. On the Saturday night preceding Hansel Monday I took the road to Aberlady in extraordinary high spirits, in anticipation of having a jolly day of it on Monday. The Sunday I spent in much the usual manner; and on Monday morning I got up out of bed about nine o'clock. The morning looked dull and raw but it was fresh and fair. As yet there was little doing out-bye; so I stayed in the house for a while, and got my breakfast and myself cleaned. About ten o'clock I stepped out the gate, and saw that some men were putting up on the sea-green two respective targets for shooting at, well superintended by about half a hundred youngsters, chiefly laddies. Two or three young fellows had congregated at the foot of the Wynd, whom I soon joined.

After the targets had been satisfactorily erected, the men and youths began to gather one by one around the shooting points. Both of those shootings, owned by different parties, were carried on under almost synonymous principles. Both used double-barrelled fowling-pieces and drops, while the rules, distance, and charge for shots were almost the same. The prizes, however, differed considerably. On the one hand, they consisted of stuffed birds; while on the other hand they were composed of – first, a pair of boots; second, a certain quantity of tobacco; and third, a grand currant loaf.

Happily, I thought I'd try my luck at the targets, so determined to have three shots at each (three shots for a shilling). At the one for stuffed birds, which I tried first, I did very little, only putting on one drop out of the three shots. Nevertheless, at the other, I put into the piece of paper one drop with my first shot, three with my second, and one with my third. My "three" was the highest score as yet, so I was quite elated, although I was almost certain that number would be exceeded before night.

By this time, the flag at the golf club was 'streaming rarely' like the 'Standard on the Braes o' Mar' long ago; and the golfers were now flocking over to the Green or Links in happy little companies, all eager to participate in the 'royal and ancient game'. One of the principal yearly competitions of the Luffness Golf Club was decided, and still is, on Hansel Monday, though very often it has had to be postponed because of the weather. On this occasion, however, the day though very cold was otherwise suitable for the competition, so a good number of members mustered at the golf club to 'mak' the roond' and try their luck.

Meanwhile, one of the younger joiner laddies had erected a rude representation of Aunt Sally on the green at the foot of the Wynd, round which the young folk were gathering fast. There I went too and had a good laugh at the lump of wood ludicrously dressed up like and old woman with a cutty pipe in her mouth. Some of my cronies and other laddies had tried to knock the pipe out of the old wife's mouth with the short cudgels for the purpose; but their attempts, with very few exceptions, proved fruitless. I was soon invited to patronise this piece of absurdity by the joiner laddie who owned it.

> "He said to me, with a grin,
> While he played three sticks a penny –
> 'Would you like to have a spin
> At my old Aunt Sally?
> I tried with every stick,
> To knock Sally on the nose,
> Forgetting quite, how quick,
> Both time and money goes,"

but I wasn't able to give her the necessary welt on the nose, so I quit the spot, and wandered away home into the house, for it was now dinner-time.

When I returned to the village green early in the afternoon, the sea had come very well into the Bay; in fact, it had encroached to within a few yards of one of the targets. The shooting was continuing at both targets with unabated vigour, and Aunt Sally was still pretty fairly patronised. But a new feature of the day was now presented on the green, namely barrow-wheeling. After having ascertained how the scores stood at the range where I had made a "3", (for, of course, I was greatly interested,) I proceeded to the barrow-wheeling starting point.

A good many youngsters and bigger laddies were gathered round the spot; and one was just getting blind-folded preparatory to his getting a trial at the barrow. He now got hold of the barrow trams, was led in a circle round the big stone that marked the starting- point, and was then placed facing the winning pin, which was some forty yards distant, and left to make his way towards it as best he could. A certain time was allowed, and the one who wheeled the barrow nearest the winning pin was, of course, the winner. You will, perhaps, suppose that it would be quite an easy matter to go straight to the pin blind-fold after being put in a direct line with it; but such is, by no means, the case. The laddie now trying it went off the course at the very first, and soon brought the wheel of the barrow in violent contact with the little dyke at the side of the road. He then turned away from the dyke, went as much off the line in an opposite direction, and was about fifteen yards on the far away side of the desired pin or peg when the cry was made that "time was up".

Well, I thought, I could surely make a better attempt at it than that, at any rate; and so handed over my penny for a fair trial. After undergoing the same manoeuvres preliminary to being let off, as I'd witnessed the other laddie undergoing, I started in a straight line for the winning pin, as I supposed. I found it a sight more awkward to have a big thick cloth tied over my eyes than I had anticipated; yet on I went confidently surmising I was going directly towards the coveted spot. When I had gone what I deemed should be about far enough, and was thinking on stopping, several exclamations came from behind me "Go on, Reidie, you're doing first-class!" So on I went a bit further, and was about to stop, when I was again stimulated to proceed by the encouraging shouts of "Go on Reidie; go on, man, and you're sure to win!" Still on, therefore, I went; but I soon felt as if my feet were in water, so I downed the barrow, and tugged the cloth off my eyes to find myself ankle deep in the sea! You may be sure I didn't stay long in that undignified predicament; but with a hop and jump at once sprung out of the water amid great shouts and laughter from the highly amused onlookers, and left the laddie who owned the wheel-barrow to get it out as best he could.

It was now getting grey gloaming, the golfers were returning from their game on the Links, blustering away about the several incidents of the day; while the men who had the shootings on the Green announced that the "ties" would need to be fired off now. I attended very assiduously at the range, where I still had a hope of

112

obtaining a prize, and was all eagerness to know the result. A "four" had been scored, so that the scorer of it was proclaimed the winner of the first prize. A number of "threes" had been put into the paper forbye my own, so that all those who had thus far succeeded, including myself, had now to fire off our "ties" for the second prize.

I put two drops into the bull's eye, the best shot among them, the rest making 'anes' and 'naethings'; but there was still a man to shoot, but wasn't at the place then. This was a well-known 'crack-shot' from Longniddry; and when he ultimately arrived and put on a "four", a score equal to the first prize winner, I yielded the second place to him without again firing. The prize I had thus won – for I was now third – was a great big currant loaf, and, I can assure you, I was mightily pleased with it and with myself into the bargain, that night.

The night fell cold, murky, and dull, yet to us younger folk the greatest treat was yet to come, and that was the Ball. The Drill Hall at the west end of the village (still there but undergoing a sad change) was the scene of this jolly dancing festival. There the young lads and lassies gathered in good force, and still better humour, a carefree, happy, and unaffected company; while all were proficient enough in their own kind of dances, and that was –

> "Nae cotillion brent new frae France,
> But country dances, strathspeys an' reels,
> Put life an' mettle in their heels!"

And had I, a laddie of fourteen summers the cheek to take a lassie to the Ball? 'Deed, had I. And more than that, I had even the cheek to take two of them! Do you think any lassie would refuse to go with a laddie who had won a prize at the shooting? H'm, ma conscience! Aye, but what about wheeling the barrow into the sea? Now, hold your tongue! They never mentioned that until I had them safely conveyed into the Drill Hall. The dancing was continued with very little or no cessation, till five or six o'clock next morning.

Thus passed Old Hansel Monday, which is not now so important a day in Aberlady as it used to be, for the customs attached to it, seem, like almost everything else, to be dying out by degrees, until very probably they 'leave not a rack behind'.

Chapter XXXVI

Days, weeks, and months sped silently away into the past on the never-tiring and unrelenting wings of time, and the genial, resuscitating Spring once more made her welcome advent. And, alas, must this be the last Spring I am fated to spend in the

113

fresh country, where the wimpling burnies, the frisking lambkins, the green budding trees, the springing corn, the returning blooms of the sweet wild-flowers, and the soothing, inspiring lilts of our dear feathered warblers, have so many fascinating charms for me? I would rather entertain the hope that that it may not be so; but - I doubt!

"An' forward tho' I cannae see,
I guess and fear."

It was now a year since I went to Ballencrieff, and, (as you'll mind, I was to try a year at the gardening), the all-important question now arose, and must be answered – was I to continue in my present vocation? My friends were almost unanimous in asserting that it would decidedly be for my benefit to try something better in the town. In this proposal I eventually acquiesced, not very easily, however, over the impending change.

With the intention of looking out for a suitable occupation, I came to Edinburgh, and thought it advisable to first seek the advice of an influential friend, the late Mr Jenkinson. I said, and he readily approved of it, that I wanted to earn a trade. It was best to have a trade, as he said, so that I might fall back on it should I try anything else and fail; and among other trades he recommended was that of a Flint Glass Cutter. Of course, I knew as much about glass-cutting than as I did about the man in the moon, and even less – though, my goodness, I certainly know more now! Mr Jenkinson possessed, in addition to his fine Glass and China Shop in Princes Street, a Glass-work in Norton Park, known as "The Edinburgh and Leith Flint Glass Company"; and, so, he fixed a time when Mr A. Jenkinson, jun., would take me through the works, and show me the different departments, so that I might form an idea myself of how I would like to work at glass-cutting.

I was, therefore, shown first through the Glass-house where they make the glass, then through the Warehouse, where I've never before seen such a fine display of glass, and then through the Cutting-shop. On being ushered into the Cutting-shop, I was quite taken aback at the sight of the flying belts, drums, spindles, etc., and the unceasing noise of the men grinding the glass on the iron wheels, or mills as we call them. Nevertheless, when I had been shown all through the shop, I thought that I could do the work very well, as I thought it would prove somewhat to my taste. On mentioning this to Mr Jenkinson he at once offered me a place there, which I took. It was on the first of May 1877 that I started my five years' apprenticeship, which expired about two months ago, so that 'my first wife's deid noo'.

As my only surviving sister was still resident in Edinburgh, and kept house here, it was agreed that I should stay with her, which I did, and do to this day. Thus, I had

114

the quiet country exchanged for the noisy bustling town, - whether for better or worse would be perhaps rather difficult to determine. I got comfortably settled down, however, and, on a whole, the town has agreed with me, and I with it, a good sight better than I anticipated – thanks, nonetheless, to the Sundays and holidays I spend out of it.

I had scarcely got started with my town life, and the new vocation of a Flint-Glass Cutter, when my much-respected grandmother, Mrs Brown, who had been ailing for some time, was taken away.

> "To that wonderland, whence tickets
> Are not issued for returning."

Yet we couldn't have expected anything else from a woman of her years; for it is the stern but necessary law of the universe –

> "So the multitude goes, like the flower
> and the weid,
> That wither away to let others succeed."

And what is this much-thought-of life of ours at the longest? But a steadily and speedily contracting span!

> "'Tis the twink of an eye, tis the draught
> of a breath,
> From the blossom of health to the
> paleness of death,
> From the gilded saloon to the bier
> and the shroud –
> O' why should the spirit of mortal
> be proud?"

At the time of her demise, my grandmother had reached the advanced age of eighty-six years, the result, or reward I may say, of a well-directed and exemplary life in her younger days. She retained all her faculties to within a short time of her death, up to which time, also, she possessed a bright and cheerful disposition. Her armchair by the fireside long appeared a sorry blank to us, where she used to sit conscientiously plying her knitting needles in making stockings, for she liked to be useful and doing, or thoughtfully perusing her well-thumbed Testament.

My father being dead, two sisters also dead, the other in Edinburgh, myself now in town, my cousin married, and now my grandmother called away, hence the "great majority" reduced that happy household to which I introduced the reader in one of my foremost chapters to a solitary individual – that my mother. Such is life!

Chapter XXXVII

Ever since I came to Old Smokie I have been in the habit of going to Aberlady almost weekly, going out on the Saturday afternoon, and returning on the Sunday night or Monday morning. I reckon myself particularly fortunate in this, as it is a happy change for a lover of Nature like myself; and it also gives some room for the scope of my little wild propensities. In this way –

> "Wi' Nature I am now estranged,
>   I ken ilk flooery hill, -
> For still they bloom as in the days
>   When we gaed to the schule,
> Thae flooers we lo'ed, thae flooers we pu'd,
>   When we gaed tae the schule."

And I thus have the opportunity of keeping up my acquaintance with the old clachan, which I shall always consider my home.

> "Hame, hoo sweet that strikes the ear,
> Hame, that word tae me sae dear,
> Hame, whaur fancy hovers near,
> Hame, sweet hame.
>
> Hame, whaur yon sweet hawthorn grows,
> Hame, whaur yon dear burnie rows,
> Hame, wi' a' yer vales an' knows,
> Hame, sweet hame.
>
> Hame, wi' a' yer hallow'd scenes,
> Favour'd nooks and auld kirk greens,
> Whaur we sported in oor "Jeans",
> Hame, sweet hame.
>
> Hame, whaur on the trees we swung,
> Hame, whaur nurs'ry rhymes were sung,
> Hame, whaur snaw-ba's aft we flung,
> Hame, sweet hame.

Oh, may I never turn my face
'Gainst thee, my ain, my native place,
Or e'er forget my kindred race,
Hame, sweet hame."

Chapter XXXVIII
(Conclusion)

There is a saying, though, perhaps, not over elegant in the minds of our more scrupulous friend's that 'everything has an end, and a puddin' has twa'. My autobiography then is like unto a pudding, it has two ends, a beginning and a conclusion. But, in another way, it differs very much from a pudding (supposing it to be a good one); in as much as the latter end of it will very like prove the most welcome.

On commencing this history of my earlier life, I never thought it would have taken me so long, or that the relating of the most prominent incidents of my boyhood (very commonplace incidents at the best), would require so many pages but, as Lord Byron says, 'stories somehow lengthen when begun'.

I have tried to describe a good number more events in much less pages but, as it is, I had to make pass over some of them when I saw they were occupying so much space and time. Some others didn't dawn on my recollection until it was too late to notify them in their proper places, so these also were left out altogether. The adventures, pliskies, explorations, pranks, and stravaigins that did rise before my memory's eye, and that I did take time and space to relate, with all their manifold faults and short-comings, have one thing to recommend them, and that is that they are written with an honest regard to truth. Some of the incidents, indeed, I may have given wrong dates, and one or two others may have been spun out or exaggerated a bit, but all the particulars are faithfully depicted, while the writer was trying, at the same time, to make them a little interesting. Of course, the dialogues had to be, necessarily, composed by myself; but, in doing so I endeavoured to give them as like the thing as possible, and, I daresay, those individuals represented therein, should any of them ever peruse these pages, will be fully persuaded that I have.

Before bringing my book altogether to a close, I have taken time to hurriedly look over the foregoing chapters, and, on a whole, I must say they don't come up to my expectations. Indeed, I thought to have done a good sight better, and there is nothing I need to be proud of. Even to my own partial judgement there are innumerable weak-points, which I am now unable to rectify or improve, so I must just crave my reader's most lenient consideration. I know full well what critics

117

would say if they were reviewing my most humble biography. They would say (even the most lenient of them) that it was a weak, crude, premature attempt at writing altogether, and the incidents were all so far-fetched, and of so little consequence, that they really were not worth the perusing, and a host of other accusations would follow that might make me hide my blushing face in a rotten's hole for the remainder of my life. But, I hope I will be exempt from such humiliation; for, as I didn't write these chapters to be published, neither did I write them to be criticized.

There is one other thing I would like to mention, and that is, how heartily disappointed I am at not writing in a purer Scotch dialect; but my vocabulary of Doric words, and my power of using even them I possessed, were far over insufficient for the occasion. I vainly attempted to adopt, and still more vainly attempted to sustain the "braid auld Scottish tongue"; and in scribbling on in that way I really felt myself labouring under a great difficulty. But, kind friends, never imagine for a moment that my admiration for our mother tongue is any less on that account. As Janet Hamilton, one of the greatest and best women Scotland has ever produced, sung in a simple and tender strain –

> "Na, na, I winna pairt wi' that,
>   I downa gie it up;
> O' Scotland's hamely mither tongue,
>   I canna quat the grup.
> It's bedded in my very heart,
>   Ye needna rive an' rug;
> It's in my e'en an' on my tongue,
>   An' singin' in my lug.
>
> "What words mair tender, kin' an' true,
>   Can wooer hae tae say,
> When doon the burn at gloamin' fa',
>   He meets his bonnie May?
> Or words mair sweet, mair saft an' dear,
>   Can lassie hae tae speak,
> When love is dancin' in her e'e,
>   An' glowin' on her cheek.
>
> "For, oh, the meltin' Doric lay,
>   In cot or clachan sung,
> The words that drap like hinney dew,
>   Frae mither Scotland's tongue,

Hae pooer tae thrill the youthfu' heart,
  An' fire the patriot's min';
Tae saften grief in ilka form,
  It comes to human kin'."

Again in Duncan McLean's words: -

"Oh! dinna droon the Doric tongue –
  Oh, dinna spurn its pooer,
The language that oor mothers sung,
  When they were in the flooer.
The hamely Doric's bune a' praise,
  It flows sweet as a rill,
It's stamped upon immortal lays
  By Burns and Tannahill!"

Or again in the words of another modern minor poet of Scotland, William Reid (not the loftier genius of William Reid of Glasgow, however); -

"My mither tongue, my mither tongue,
  Tho' grander speech there be,
An' lowly is thy hame attire,
  You're dearer far tae me,
Than flauntin' speech in gandy dress,
  That poet ever sung;
What words can gang aboot the heart,
  Sae warm's the mither tongue.

"The mither tongue, the mither tongue,
  The first we try tae learn,
The words come sweetly on mine ear,
  I lispit when a bairn:
In schule-boy days we English gat,
  An' by oor auld Scotch flung,
But schule-hours past, an' oot tae play,
  We spak' oor mither tongue."

An once again, I can't resist the temptation of quoting a bit of what J. Logie-Robertson says on "The Decadence of the Scots Language, Customs, etc." –

119

"Weel could it a oor wants express,
Weel could it ban, weel could it bless;
Wi' a' oor feelin's 'twas acquent,
Had words for pleasure and complent;
Was sweet tae hear in sacred psalm,
In simmer Sabbath's mornin' calm;
An' at the family exerceese,
When auld guidman, on bended knees,
Wrastled, as Jacob did langsyne,
For favours temporal an' divine.

"'Twas mair sonorous than the latin,
Cam' heavier on the hide o' Satan,
When frae his Abel o' a poopit,
The minister grew hearse an' roopit,
An' bann'd wi' energetic jaw,
The author o' the primal fa'.
But gin the poopit's sacred clangour
Was something awesome in its anger,
Gude keep my Soothlan' freens frae hearin'
A rouch red-heided Scotchman swearin'!
But wha wad hae audacity
Tae question its capacity?

"The guid braid Scots! – a language still,
Let fortune vary as she will.
'Tho' banished fae oor College ha's,
It frames the siccar auld Scots laws;
Tho' frae the lips, o' speech the portal,
It lives in Literature immortal.
But, oh, alas! the waifu' change,
The customs new, the fashions strange,
Sin' the auld patriarchal days
O' sober thocht and simple phrase!"

But in literature, I think the old Doric is more adapted to poetry and song, than to prose works of any length. Nonetheless, there are a few prose works of considerable length, well sustained in happy Doric; as bear witness "Mansie Wauch", and "Tammas Bodkin", which I would recommend to all who enjoy a good Scotch story. And, moreover, there are, I rejoice to say, a good many of our living *litterateurs* who write admirable prose sketches in that dialect, notably our modern Scottish wit, bauld Robin Ford as "Surfaceman" (Alex Anderson) calls him. In the hands of such men as he, and many more I could name, I hope the old

Scots will long live, and be prolifically used in its purest simplicity and expressiveness.

But now, to come to a close, I trust my little homely, unambitious book may prove of a little interest, and afford a little amusement to a few friends and cronies; and if it accomplishes that end, the author will hold himself sufficiently recompensed for his time and trouble.

THE END

Author's Note:

I am now given to understand that there are some blunders in the third chapter about some of the particulars of our family history. However, they are not, in my opinion, of very great consequence: and, moreover, it was not on these points I intended to write, so I shall not try to correct or point out my mistakes, as in doing so I might very probably be told I had just made the more! I hope those of my readers who are better acquainted with these particulars than I am myself will kindly overlook my said hallucinations, and those who are not acquainted with them will oblige by being not over credulous when perusing this particular chapter.

We regret to record the death which occurred at his residence "Sunnybrae", Aberlady on Wednesday morning after a long illness of Mr John Pringle Reid, market gardener. Deceased, who was 68 years of age, was a native of Aberlady but in his early years went to Edinburgh where he practiced his trade as a glasscutter. Later, he established a china merchant's business in the city, and about 27 years ago, returned to his native village to take up market gardening. He established the firm of J P Reid & Co and was well known in his profession throughout Scotland. Of a popular and kindly disposition, Mr Reid entered loyally into all good movements connected with the village, and was ever ready to lend a helping hand for any good cause. As an author, Mr Reid occupied an honoured place in East Lothian. He published a number of books among them being a volume of poems, most of which had appeared in the columns of the Courier, entitled "Facts and Fancies". He was the author of "The Skippers' Daughters", a novel of great interest and full of local colour. Mr Reid was greatly interested in the folklore and history of the village and neighbourhood and from his pen came a "Guide to Aberlady" which contains a valuable collection of historical anecdote. "The Skipper's Daughters" was dramatised by Mr Reid and was performed with outstanding success by the Aberlady Dramatic Society. A number of years ago, Mr Reid was a frequent contributor to the old-established publication the "People's Friend". He had keenly at heart the welfare of his native village, and he never turned a deaf ear to any appeal made for his help, if the object were worthy. He was vice-president of the Bowling Club, and was connected with the Curling Club for many years. Mr Reid was the means of resuscitating the Aberlady Horticultural Society, after its war-time lapse and, as secretary, worked hard for the success of the Annual Flower Show - one of the most important of such exhibitions in East Lothian. He was the founder of the Aberlady Dramatic Society, an organisation which has given much enjoyment and helped several charities in the district. Deceased was a keen member of the Burns Club, and took a "special interest" in the children's competitions under the auspices of that body, on many occasions giving prizes or acting as a judge. In earlier days, Mr Reid was a member of the Aberlady Company of the Volunteers, and was one time president of the Miniature Rifle Club. Mr Reid had a connection with the Courier which lasted over a quarter of a century, and on many occasions readers were treated to little cameos in prose and verse that reflected the home-kindly heart of the man, whom to know was respect and admire. He is survived by his widow and a son and daughter, to whom the deep sympathy of a wide circle of friends is extended.